TAKE A BANDANA

16 BEAUTIFUL PROJECTS FOR YOUR HOME

TAKE A BANDANA

16 BEAUTIFUL PROJECTS FOR YOUR HOME

Jemima Schlee

THE GUILD OF MASTER CRAFTSMAN
PUBLICATIONS

First published 2015 by
Guild of Master Craftsman Publications Ltd
Castle Place, 166 High Street, Lewes,
East Sussex BN7 1XU

Text © Jemima Schlee, 2015

Copyright in the Work © GMC Publications Ltd, 2015

ISBN 978 1 86108 788 1

Publisher Jonathan Bailey
Production Manager Jim Bulley
Senior Project Editor Virginia Brehaut
Editor Nicola Hodgson
Managing Art Editor Gilda Pacitti
Photography Andrew Perris
Additional Photography Holly Joliffe
(pages 12, 14, 17, 49 and 57)
Step Photography Jemima Schlee

Colour origination by GMC Reprographics
Printed and bound in China

For Harrison and Martha

Contents

Needle Case p.42

Fabric Card Holder p.78

Covered Coat Hanger p.100

Patchwork Pincushion p.28

INTRODUCTION

Worn by pirates, labourers and pioneers of the Wild West for hundreds

of years, the bandana is a dressing-up box staple – making an instant

dandy, fop, gypsy, magician, buccaneer or cowboy.

Bandanas are both practical and useful. Referred to in the 18th century as 'little banners', they were printed with words and images to commemorate, celebrate and advertise. Their main purpose was to convey information, ideas and messages.

The American bandana has become an iconic accessory of the cowboy, used as a handkerchief, a neck scarf, as protection from the sun, sand and dust, or as an impromptu wrapping for possessions, a mask, a bandage, or a sling…

From its image in the Wild, Wild West to a fashion statement today, the basic size and design of bandanas has altered little over the centuries. Here are 16 practical, timeless items for your home and garden for you to make from bandanas.

The traditional style of paisley borders, illustrations and spots are instantly familiar, nostalgic and festive.

This page: Patchwork
Pincushion **page 28**
Opposite: Knitting-needle
Purse **page 36**

This page: Wreath
page 56
Opposite: Needle Case
page 42

This page: Flag **page** 48
Opposite: Knitting Bag **page** 32

This page: Notebook
Cover **page 68**
Opposite: Pinwheel
Picnic Cloth **page 60**

Opposite: Quilt **page 104**
This page: Fabric Card Holder **page 78**

This page: Covered Coat Hanger **page 100**
Opposite: Shoe Bags **page 96**

This page: Bunting
page 52
Opposite: Shopping-bag
Tidy **page 84**

This page: Nightdress
Case **page 92**
Opposite: Camera Strap
page 72

THE WORKROOM

This is a great project for using up scraps, as you can make the pincushions any size. I like to keep one for pins, one for small needles and one for larger needles. By using a window template, careful selection of the patterns or motifs can create many different designs.

Supplies:

- ☐ Scraps of bandanas or other fabric of your choice
- ☐ Backing fabric 9½in (24cm) square
- ☐ Cotton or hollowfibre stuffing or wadding
- ☐ 2 buttons ⅜–½in (1–1.25cm) in diameter
- ☐ Pencil or pen

- ☐ Scissors
- ☐ Needle, pins and thread
- ☐ Sewing machine
- ☐ Iron
- ☐ Long embroidery or sewing needle
- ☐ Embroidery thread

Step 1
Photocopy and cut out the templates from page 128. Use window templates (see page 114) so that you can position them carefully on your bandana scraps. In this way, you can cut similar parts of the patterns for each patch. You will need to cut six segments from bandana scraps and one circle from backing fabric for each pincushion. Working with the six segments first, place two pieces of fabric right sides together and pin or tack along one long edge. Stitch a ⅜in (1cm) seam by machine, remove the pins or tacking and press the seam open.

Step 2
Take a third patch and place it right sides together on top of the two joined pieces, aligning it with one of the segments. Pin or tack along the corresponding long raw edges.

Step 3
Stitch a ⅜in (1cm) seam by machine, remove the pins or tacking and press it open with a hot iron.

Step 4
Repeat this process to join the remaining three patches until you have two semi-circles with their seams pressed open. Trim any uneven edges with sharp scissors. Lay the two halves right sides together and pin or tack along the long edge.

Step 5
Stitch a ⅜in (1cm) seam by machine, remove the pins or tacking and press the seam open with a hot iron. Place the patched circle down, right side up. Lay the plain backing circle right side down centred on top of it, and pin the two layers together. Trim the patched circle flush all the way around to match the size of the backing circle.

Step 6
Stitch a ⅜in (1cm) seam around the edge of the two circles, leaving a 2in (5cm) turning gap. Start and finish with reverse stitch to strengthen the edges.

Step 7
Use scissors to trim the fabric to ⅛in (3mm) from the outside stitch line, but not at the turning gap to avoid fraying. Turn your work right side out, tease the circular seam so that it is crisp, and press with a hot iron. Stuff firmly with wadding or stuffing.

Step 8
Turn in the raw edges of the turning gap and close it with small overstitches by hand (see page 123).

Step 9
Thread 44in (112cm) of doubled embroidery thread onto the long needle and knot the ends. Push the needle through the centre of the stuffed pincushion, then back through the same way again so that the thread runs around the outside edge of the pincushion along one of the patch joins.

Step 10
Repeat a further five times so that your pincushion is divided into six segments. Pull the threads taut to create the plump segments. Thread the needle back through so that both thread ends are on the same side and knot off tightly to maintain the definition of the segments. Trim three of the four thread ends to ⅜in (1cm) and tuck the raw ends into one of the segment folds. Use the final thread to stitch a button to the centre of either side.

Step 11
Finally, make a few small stitches under the button on the back of the pincushion to finish off.

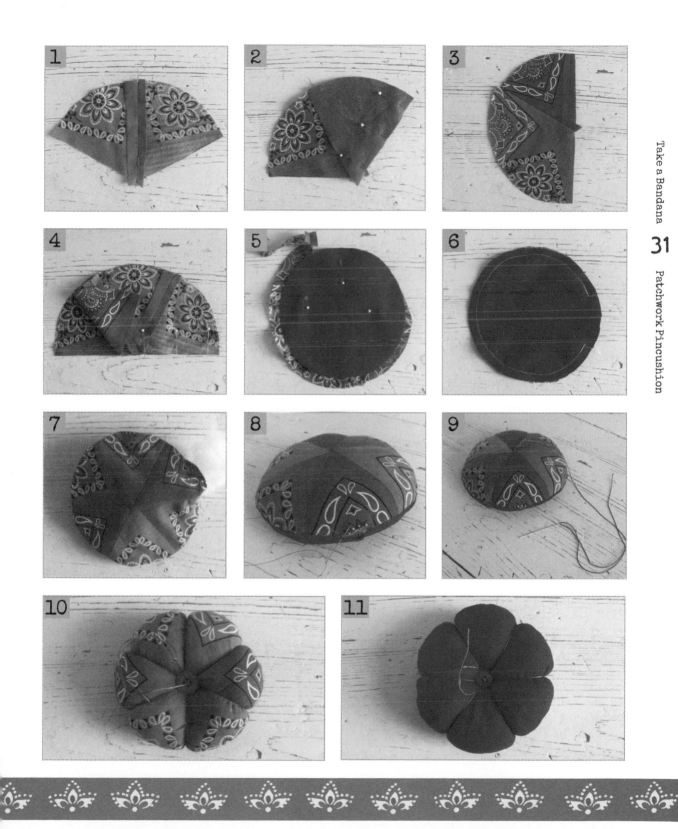

The design of this useful bag was inspired by the memory of one my grandmother always carried with her. Pack away your knitting, with an extra ball or two of yarn, into a capacious, classic bag – perfect for travelling or just for tucking away under a cushion.

KNITTING BAG

Supplies:

- [ ] Two bandanas, each a minimum of 18in (46cm) square, or fabric of your choice cut to this measurement
- [ ] 18 x 36in (46 x 91.5cm) linen or cotton for lining
- [ ] Four small buttons
- [ ] Pair of 7in (18cm) wooden bag handles

- [ ] Scissors
- [ ] Needle and pins
- [ ] Threads to match the fabrics
- [ ] Sewing machine
- [ ] Iron
- [ ] Zipper foot

Step 1

Lay the two bandanas out, right sides together, and trim them if necessary, so that they are the same size. If you have any raw edges, zigzag stitch along them to reduce fraying. Pin or tack along the two sides and along the edge nearest to you – the unpinned edge furthest from you will be the top opening of your bag. Mark a point halfway down on both sides. Starting at one of these halfway points, stitch a ⅜in (1cm) seam by machine down to the bottom corner, along the bottom edge, and back up to the opposite halfway point, reverse stitching at either end. Remove the pins or tacking and trim the two bottom corners at a 90-degree angle, close to the stitch line. Press the seams open.

Step 2

Fold the lining fabric in half, right sides together; the folded edge is the bottom of the lining. Pin or tack up the two sides so that the raw edges align. Mark a point on each side seam halfway up from the bottom edge minus ⅜in (1cm). Starting at these marks, stitch a ⅜in (1cm) seam down to the bottom folded edge, reverse stitching at either end. Remove the pins or tacking and trim the two bottom corners at a 45-degree angle close to the stitch line. Press the seams open.

Step 3

Turn the lining right side out and place it inside the outer bandanas (which remain inside out). Align all the raw edges and the side seams, and pin or tack.

Step 4

Mark a 6in (15cm) turning gap at the top centre of one side of the bag. Starting on one side of the turning gap, stitch a ⅜in (1cm) seam all the way

TIP

USING DIFFERENT PROPORTIONS, YOU COULD MAKE THIS INTO A CUTE LITTLE HANDBAG INSTEAD.

around. Stop as you reach the point halfway along one side seam, working up to the stitching point from Step 2, and reverse stitch before breaking off. Start again on the other side of the halfway point, reverse stitching at the beginning, working all the way around to the halfway point on the other side, and reverse stitching again when you finish. Finally, work the last seam starting from the other side of the turning gap and working along and down to the halfway point. Remove the pins or tacking and trim the four top corners at a 90-degree angle close to the stitch line. Carefully ease the bag right side out through the turning gap.

Step 5

Tease and manipulate the layers so that you have a good crisp edge all around the two sides of the top opening before pressing with a hot iron. Turn in the raw edges of the turning gap by ⅜in (1cm). Close the turning gap by hand with overstitch.

Step 6

Place the bag down in front of you and turn the top edge down. Now fold the back top edge down by 2½in (6cm), pin and press.

Step 7

Slip one of the wooden handles under the right-hand corner of the fold. First pin and then tack the fold back down into its previous position, making sure you stitch through all the layers of fabric.

Step 8

Work methodically across the top of the bag, bunching the fabric you have already tacked to the right-hand side of the handle as you go, until the whole of the top edge is wrapped over the bottom of the handle. Using a zipper foot, machine stitch a hem ⅛in (3mm) in from the edge, and another ⅜in (1cm) below the bottom of the handle. These lines of sewing will be a bit fiddly; keep the fabric layers as flat as possible as they pass under the needle. Take it slowly, stopping if necessary, with the needle down, to raise the foot and rearrange the fabric.

Step 9

Sew a pair of small buttons, one on the inside and one on the outside, just below the halfway mark on either side of the bag, centred on the side seams. Sandwich the fabric layers between them.

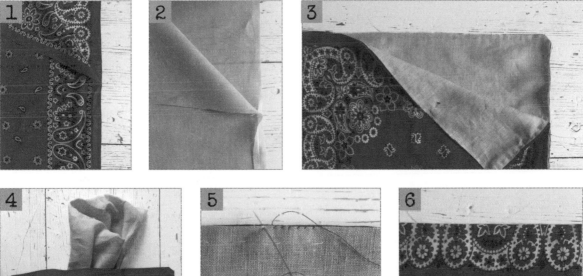

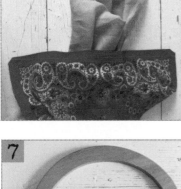

This long purse can be used to store knitting needles. You could adapt the pattern to include pockets on the inside, or make a shorter purse to hold crochet hooks. I use a 6in (15cm)-deep version to carry a small sewing kit when I'm travelling.

Supplies:

- [ ] One bandana, minimum dimensions 18in (46cm) square, or fabric of your choice cut to those measurements
- [ ] 18in (46cm) square linen or cotton for lining
- [ ] 18in (46cm) square of cotton wadding
- [ ] 18in (46cm) square of fusible interfacing
- [ ] 5½in (14cm) glue-in purse frame
- [ ] Scissors
- [ ] Sewing needle and pins
- [ ] Sewing machine
- [ ] Threads to match the fabrics
- [ ] Iron
- [ ] Fabric glue

Step 1

Cut two pattern pieces (see template on page 129) from the bandana, lining fabric, wadding and the fusible interfacing. Fuse the wadding to the wrong sides of the bandana pieces using an iron and the fusible web. Place the two pieces of padded bandana right sides together, and pin or tack along the sides and bottom edges.

Step 2

Sew a $\frac{1}{2}$in (1.25cm) seam by machine, starting at one hinge-position mark (indicated on the pattern) and continuing around the outer edge until you reach the next mark, leaving the top section open. Reverse stitch at the start and finish to strengthen. Trim the two bottom corners at 45 degrees, making sure you don't snip the stitching.

Step 3

Press the seams open. Working on one of the bottom corners, create a box corner (see page 122) by putting your hand inside the lining and pushing the fabric out away from the seam. Align the side seam exactly with the bottom seam and press flat so that the corner forms a triangle. Sew across 1in (2.5cm) from the tip of the corner several times. Trim the seam to $\frac{1}{8}$in (3mm). Repeat with the other bottom corner.

Step 4

Place the two pieces of lining fabric right sides together and pin or tack around the side and bottom edges.

Step 5

Stitch a $\frac{1}{2}$in (1.25cm) seam from one hinge-position mark to the other (the long way), leaving a turning gap of $2\frac{3}{4}$in (7cm) along the bottom seam. Reverse stitch at the start and finish to strengthen.

Step 6

Press the seams open and make box corners as you did at Step 3 for the bandana outer.

TIP

MAKE YOUR OWN PATTERN TO FIT A PURSE FRAME. DRAW A HORIZONTAL LINE AND LAY THE FRAME ON IT SO THAT THE HINGES ARE CENTRED. DRAW A LINE ALONG THE INSIDE CURVE FROM ONE HINGE TO THE OTHER. DRAW ANOTHER PENCIL LINE $\frac{1}{2}$IN (1.25CM) OUTSIDE THE SHAPE YOU HAVE JUST DRAWN. THIS FORMS THE TOP OF THE PATTERN. DRAW $11\frac{1}{2}$IN (29CM) VERTICAL LINES EXTENDING DOWN FROM THE TWO HINGE POINTS THEN A HORIZONTAL LINE AT THE BOTTOM TO JOIN THEM.

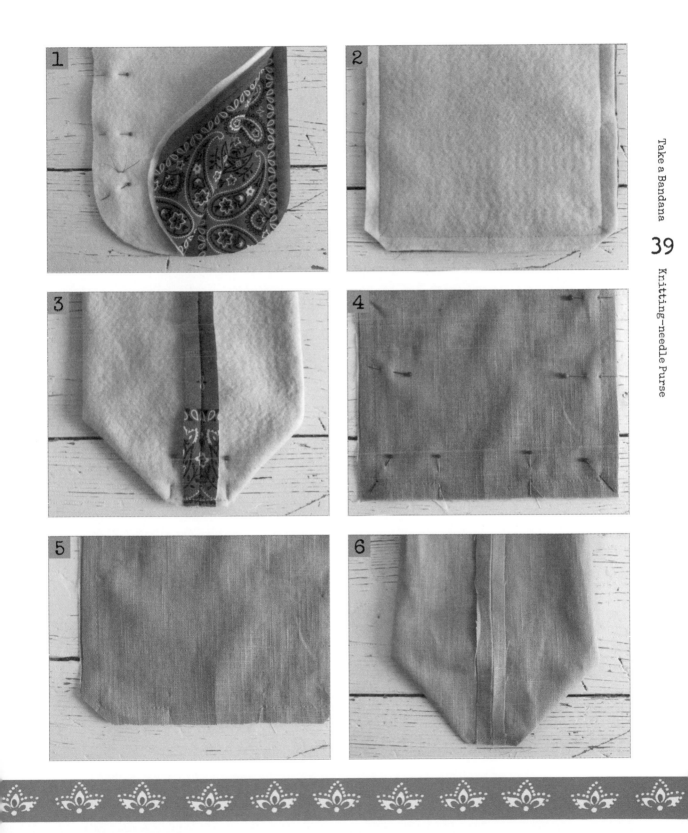

TIP

IF YOU WANT TO MAKE A FIRMER VERSION OF THIS PURSE, USE TWO PIECES OF HEAVY ADHESIVE STIFFENER (DESIGNED FOR CURTAIN PELMETS) BETWEEN THE WADDING AND THE BANDANA FABRIC. CUT THE PIECES USING THE BASIC PATTERN SHAPE, THEN TRIM $3/8$IN (1CM) ALL THE WAY AROUND BEFORE FIXING IT TO THE OUTER FABRIC WITH AN IRON, FOLLOWING THE MANUFACTURER'S INSTRUCTIONS.

Step 7

Cut notches at the hinge points marked on the pattern on both the outer and the lining pieces, just where the stitching starts and ends.

Step 8

Turn the lining piece right side out, place it inside the outer bandana piece (still inside out) and align all the edges and the side seams carefully. Pin or tack around the top opening to hold the lining and outer piece in position before sewing.

Step 9

Starting at the top centre of one side, stitch a ½in (1.25cm) seam all the way around the opening. Stop at the side seams with the needle down, raise the foot and manipulate your work under it so that you can continue without breaking the stitching. Clip small V-shapes near to but not through the seams along the top curves.

Step 10

Carefully ease the purse right side out through the turning gap in the lining. Slipstitch the turning gap closed by hand using overstitch (see page 123).

Step 11

With the lining pushed back inside the bandana outer, tease and manipulate the layers so that you have a good crisp edge all around the top opening. Pin or tack it before topstitching ⅛in (3mm) in from the edge.

Step 12

Run a line of fabric glue along the inside of one half of the frame, starting and stopping a few millimetres from the hinge at either side. Do the same along one side of the purse opening, starting and stopping ⅜in (1cm) from each side seam. Insert the fabric into the frame. Take care that the sides are at similar levels first, then feed the centre in. Use your fingers or a small crochet hook to push the fabric in snugly and to make sure that the line of topstitching is hidden within the frame. Leave to dry fully before gluing the other side.

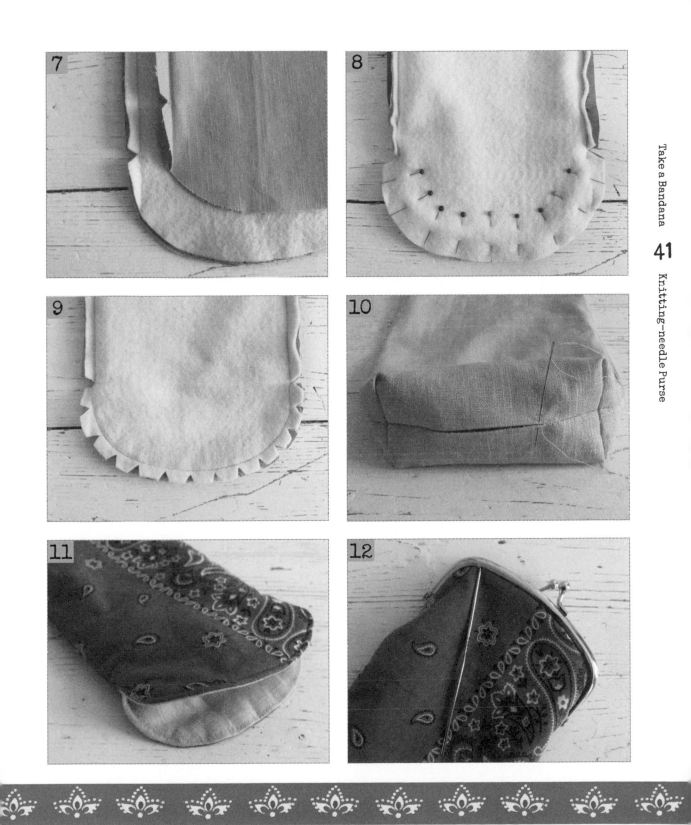

A needle case is ideal for keeping sewing, embroidery and darning needles safe, particularly when travelling. This simple one has four linen 'pages' for needles and a magnet set in the centre of the front cover to corral them while you work.

NEEDLE CASE

Supplies:

- One bandana, minimum dimensions 18in (46cm) square, or fabric of your choice cut to those measurements
- 8 x 4in (20 x 10cm) of fusible interfacing
- 8 x 4in (20 x 10cm) of cotton wadding
- 8 x 4in (20 x 10cm) heavyweight iron-on stiffener
- Six buttons ⅜in (1cm) in diameter or smaller
- Three pieces of 8 x 3½in (20 x 9cm) white linen

- 4¾in (12cm) of 1in (2.5cm)-wide white herringbone tape
- Circular adhesive magnets ⅜in (1cm) in diameter for fastening (optional)
- Scissors
- Iron
- Sewing machine
- Needle and pins
- Threads to match the fabrics
- Pinking shears

Step 1

Cut a strip of bandana measuring 4¾ x 18in (12 x 46cm). Cut the wadding and fusible interfacing into two 4in (10cm) squares. Fuse each wadding square to a square of fusible interfacing with an iron. Cut the stiffener into two equal squares measuring 4 x 3⅞in (10 x 9.5cm) and one narrow strip measuring 4 x ¼in (10cm x 5mm). Lay the bandana piece down in front of you wrong side up. Fuse the narrow strip of stiffener to it with an iron, positioning it exactly on the centre of the fabric with equal spaces above and below it. Then fuse the two pieces of cotton wadding on either side, leaving a ¼in (5mm) gap between them and the thin strip.

Step 2

Turn your work over. Fold each side in along the edges of the cotton wadding and press. Now fold the two raw short edges at the centre back on themselves by ¼in (5mm) and press. Lay the herringbone tape down the centre, aligning the top and bottom edges with the fabric and covering the folded edges. Pin or tack along the top edge to hold everything in position.

Step 3

Pin or tack the bottom edges and the bottom end of the herringbone tape. Stitch ⅜in (1cm) seams along the top and bottom edges, reverse stitching at the beginning and ends of both seams. Trim the four corners close to, but not cutting, the stitching at 45 degrees. Do the same with the ends of the herringbone tape to reduce bulk.

Step 4

Working through the gaps underneath the tape, turn your work right side out and flip the tape to the other side so that it lies underneath the two folded edges. Use a pin to ease the corners out and make them nice and sharp.

Step 5

Press with a hot iron. Slip the two pieces of stiffener into the two pockets with the 4in (10cm) measurement lying vertically. Make sure that the 'glue' sides are facing as you do so.

Step 6

With the stiffener pushed firmly into the corners of their pockets, fuse them to the fabric with a hot iron. Tack down the folded edges where they overlap the tape, thus enclosing the stiffener, and topstitch by machine very close to the edge.

Step 7

Trim the edges of the linen pieces with pinking shears. Fold them in half and press to find the centre. Open them out again and lay them on your main piece with the crease lying down the middle of the herringbone tape. Anchor the linen to the outer with pairs of buttons – one on the inside and one on the outside – sandwiching all the layers of fabric and tape in between.

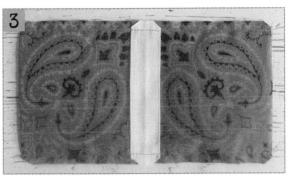

TIP

YOU CAN ADD ADHESIVE MAGNETS TO THE CENTRE OF THE TWO PIECES OF STIFFENER BEFORE STEP 5. MAKE SURE THEY ARE NOT ATTACHED TO THE 'GLUE' SIDE.

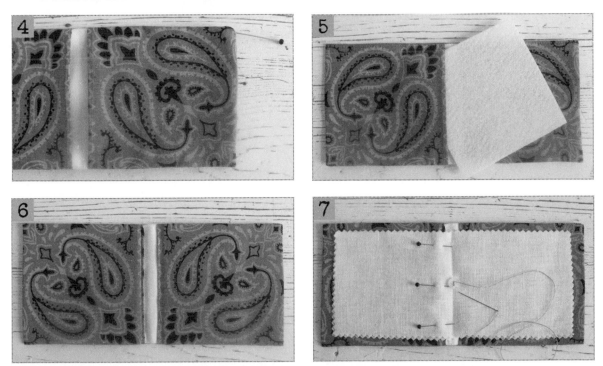

THE VERANDA

Celebrate summer, spring, holidays, birthdays, anniversaries, or even just lunch! Just like bunting, a flag makes any occasion special. This flag can be made in any simple or complicated assortment of colours – keep it simple with just two colours, or use up all your scraps from other projects.

FLAG

Supplies:

- ☐ Three bandanas, a minimum of 18in (46cm) square, or fabrics of your choice cut to this measurement, two in matching or similar colours and one in a contrasting colour
- ☐ 36in (91.5cm) of 1in (2.5cm)-wide white herringbone tape
- ☐ 42in (106cm) of piping cord
- ☐ 1¼in (3cm) wooden toggle

- ☐ White thread and thread to match main colours of the bandanas
- ☐ Pencil or air-erasable pen
- ☐ Ruler
- ☐ Measuring tape
- ☐ Scissors
- ☐ Sewing needle and pins
- ☐ Sewing machine
- ☐ Iron

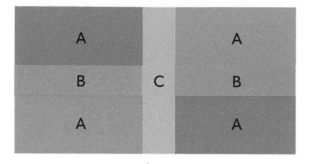

PREPARING THE PATTERN PIECES
Cut four pieces of bandana 13¾ x 8¾in (35 x 22cm) for the four corner rectangles (see A on diagram). These need to be the same, or similar, colours. Cut two pieces 13¾ x 4in (35 x 10cm) (B), and one piece 17½ x 4in (44.5 x 10cm) (C) for the cross. These need to be in a contrasting colour to the rectangles. Lay the pieces out in their correct positions to one side so that you don't confuse the fabric sections when you are piecing them together.

Step 1
Take the top left-hand A piece and pin or tack its long edge to the long edge of the left-hand B piece with wrong sides together. Machine-stitch a ⅜in (1cm) seam. Trim the seam edge of piece A down to half its depth.

Step 2
Press the seam towards piece A, tucking under the overhang of piece B, encasing the raw edge of piece A and forming a clean fell fold hem (see page 118). Topstitch ⅛in (3mm) from the folded edge.

Step 3
Repeat this process to attach the bottom left-hand panel. Do the same with the three right-hand pieces.

Step 4
Now attach both of these to the central piece C using the same type of enclosed hems.

Step 5
Hem three sides of the flag, leaving one short end raw. Use an iron to fold the three edges ¼in (5mm) over, then ¼in (5mm) again. Stitch ⅛in (3mm) from the edge. Change the thread for each colour.

Step 6
Fold one end of the piping cord 6in (15cm) from one end and use a zigzag stitch to secure the raw end in place. Tie the toggle 4¾in (12cm) from the other end of the piping cord and secure the raw end with zigzag stitch.

Step 7
Lay the unhemmed edge of the flag along the herringbone tape, aligning it with the centre of the tape's width. Tack the flag edge to the centre of the tape. Fold in both ends of the tape about 1½in (4cm) to encase the corners of the flag at the top and bottom and pin or tack them in place. Lay the piping cord along the centre of the tape so that the toggle protrudes at the top, and the loop at the bottom.

Step 8
Fold the tape in half lengthways, press, and pin or tack it to hold it in position, ensuring that the edges of the tape are aligned on either side of the flag. Make sure that the piping cord runs freely in the channel created by the tape, apart from where it is attached near the top. Stitch ⅛in (3mm) from the edge, reversing the stitching at both ends for strength.

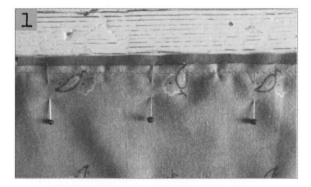

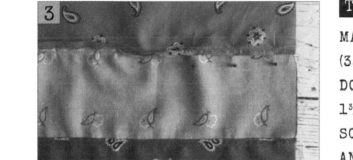

TIP

MAKE A FLAGPOLE USING $1^3/_8$IN (3.5CM)-DIAMETER WOODEN DOWELLING TOPPED OFF WITH A $1^3/_8$IN (3.5CM) WOODEN DOOR HANDLE, SCREWED ON THROUGH ITS CENTRE AND REINFORCED WITH SOME GLUE.

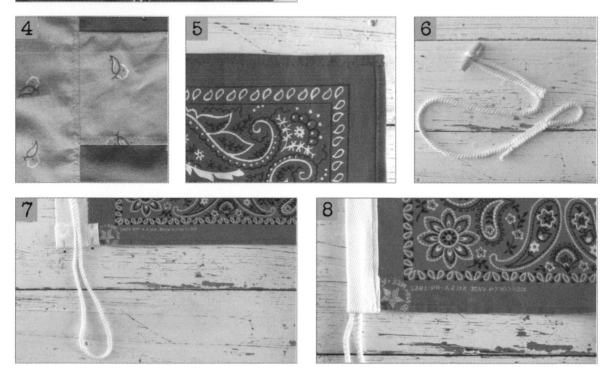

Bunting makes it party time, any time. Hang it up inside or outside to create an instantly happy atmosphere. These flags are double-sided for extra durability. This is a great project for using up scraps; you can add to it, make smaller or larger versions, or adapt it using different shapes.

BUNTING

Supplies:

To make 170in (4.35m) of bunting:

- ☐ Three bandanas 18in (46cm) square, or fabric of your choice cut to those measurements (one bandana makes five flags)
- ☐ 180in (4.6m) of ¾in (2cm)-wide cotton herringbone or bunting tape
- ☐ Scissors
- ☐ Sewing needles and pins
- ☐ Sewing machine
- ☐ White cotton thread
- ☐ Iron
- ☐ Thread to match the base colour of your bandanas

Step 1

Use the template on page 130 to cut out the flag shapes from the bandanas. Each 18in (46cm)-square bandana will make five flags. Take two triangles and place them right sides together, aligning all three raw edges. Pin or tack along the two long sides and stitch a ⅜in (1cm) seam along both these sides, turning at the pointed tip by leaving the sewing-machine needle down, raising the foot and pivoting your work before lowering the foot again. Reverse stitch at the beginning and end for extra strength. Trim the bottom point of your 'flag' to lessen the bulk when you turn it out.

Step 2

Turn the flag right side out. Tease and manipulate the seams to make them sharp. Press with a hot iron and topstitch ⅛in (3mm) in from the edge of the two long sides with thread to match the base colour of your bandana. Trim along the top of the flag to give it an even raw edge. Make the rest of your flags – 15 in total.

Step 3

Take one end of the herringbone tape and fold it in 4¾in (12cm) on itself. Now fold in the raw end of the tape and zigzag stitch back and forth several times. This creates a loop at the end of the tape to make hanging the bunting quick and easy. Do the same with the other end.

Step 4

Fold the tape all the way along between the two loops to make it ½in (1.25cm) wide and press with a hot iron. Starting 6in (15cm) from the left-hand loop, slot the flags snugly into the fold of the tape and pin or tack into place with gaps of roughly 4¾in (12cm) between them, alternating the colours as you go.

Step 5

Starting at one end, stitch along the open edge of the folded tape all the way from the base of one loop to the other, thus closing the tape and attaching all the flags.

TIP

MAKE A QUICK VERSION OF THIS BUNTING BY SEWING THE FLAGS WITH A SINGLE THICKNESS OF FABRIC, FOLDING THE TWO LONG EDGES OVER AT STEP 2 AND ZIGZAG STITCHING ALONG THE RAW EDGES TO MAKE A HEM. THE FINISHED RESULT WON'T BE AS STURDY, AND PROBABLY WON'T BECOME A FAMILY HEIRLOOM, BUT WILL TAKE YOU A FRACTION OF THE TIME TO MAKE.

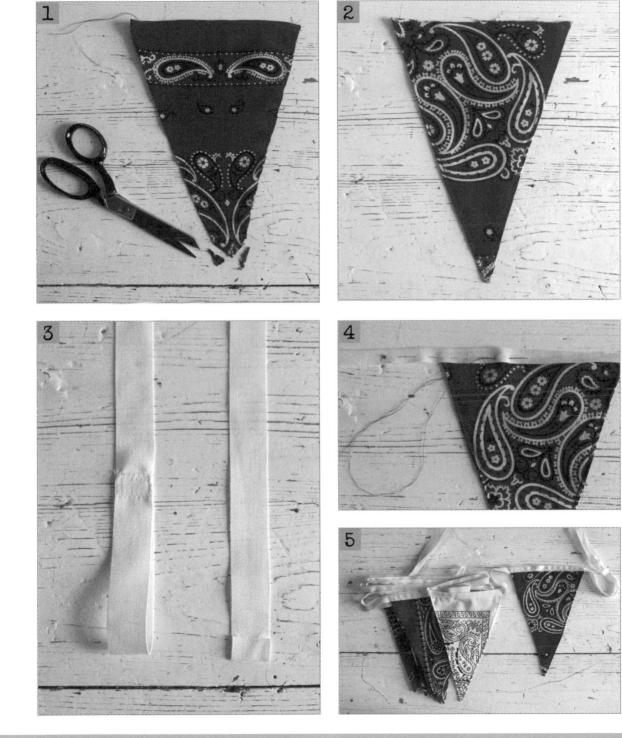

An all-seasons decoration for outside or inside, this wreath uses up all your little scraps of bandana fabric. Make one in tones and shades of a single colour, or mix complementary colours for vibrancy. This is a very simple, quick project that does not involve any sewing.

WREATH

Supplies:

To make a wreath roughly 16in (40cm) in diameter
(although you can make this project any size you like):

☐ Scraps of bandanas (and plain cotton scraps to make up any deficit), or other fabric scraps of your choice

☐ 12in (30cm) embroidery hoop

☐ Acrylic paint and paintbrush (optional)

☐ Scissors

☐ Found items such as pine cones or shells to accessorize your wreath (see tip box overleaf)

Step 1

The smallest of fabric pieces can be used to make this wreath, so whenever you make a project, always keep your scraps of fabric – I keep mine in an old galvanized bucket. Before you start, tip all your scraps onto your worktable and play around grouping them – contrasting colours, brights and monochromes – then decide which scraps you are going to use.

Step 2

Take your embroidery hoop apart and put the part with the screw fixing to one side. Don't waste it though; you can use it to make another wreath, just tighten the screw and cover it with fabric as you tie the scraps on at step 3. Paint the ring with acrylic paint if you want to. One coat is probably enough as you will aim to cover it with fabric.

Step 3

Cut any larger scraps down to size – the pieces should be an average of 6in (15cm) long, and no more than 1½in (4cm) wide, but their actual shape is not important, nor their raw edges. Tie the scraps around your wooden circle, taking time to make sure you are happy with the positions of the different colours and tones.

Step 4

Continue tying on scraps until the hoop is completely covered. Over time, if left outside, the cotton fabric scraps will weather in the sun and fray in the wind, adding beautiful character to your wreath.

TIP

THINK ABOUT ACCESSORIZING YOUR WREATH. PERHAPS SOME SEASONAL EXTRAS SUCH AS TWIGS AND PINE CONES IN THE AUTUMN, SHELLS IN THE SUMMER, BAUBLES AT CHRISTMAS, AND LEAVES AND BLOSSOMS IN THE SPRING. TIE ON FOUND OBJECTS FROM ALL SEASONS TO CREATE, OVER TIME, A WREATH FULL OF MEMORIES.

TIP

LAY THE SCRAPS OUT IN A LARGE
CIRCLE AND PLAY AROUND WITH THE
ORDER OF THE COLOURS BEFORE
YOU START TYING THEM ON. THIS
IS A PROJECT THAT CAN BE KEPT IN
PROGRESS, AS YOU COMPLETE OTHER
PROJECTS AND ACCUMULATE SCRAPS.

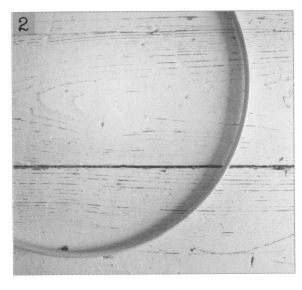

Make a bright picnic cloth or tablecloth with a patched 'pinwheel' border. Alter the dimensions to suit your needs by adding to the width and length by increments of 10in (25cm). Make this cloth with various tones of light and dark bandanas to ensure the pinwheel pattern stands out clearly.

PINWHEEL PICNIC CLOTH

Supplies:

To make a 44in (112cm) square cloth:

- ☐ Two pink bandanas 18in (46cm) square, or fabric of your choice cut to those measurements
- ☐ Two turquoise bandanas 18in (46cm) square, or fabric of your choice cut to this measurement (Note: your bandanas need not be exactly the same shade or pattern)
- ☐ 48in (122cm) square of plain linen
- ☐ 5½yds (5m) of bias binding to either match or contrast with the plain linen

- ☐ Scissors
- ☐ Sewing needles and pins
- ☐ Iron
- ☐ Pencil or air-erasable pen
- ☐ Sewing machine
- ☐ Thread to match the linen
- ☐ Threads to match the base colour of your bandanas

Step 1

Use template A on page 130 to cut out triangles from the bandanas. You should be able to get up to 18 from each bandana, and you will need 32 in each of your two colours. Take care to make sure the long edge of the triangle template is placed on the bias of your fabric (see tip).

Step 2

Place two triangles right sides together, aligning all three raw edges. Pin or tack along the long edge and stitch a ⅜in (1cm) seam along this edge. Press the seam open with a hot iron.

Step 3

Use template B on page 130 to square off the two-patch square. Place it on top of the patch, aligning its diagonal with the pressed seam – use the red diagonal line on the template to help you do this. Draw around the square and then trim the edges with sharp scissors, leaving a neat square with no extra fabric at the ends of the diagonal seam.

Step 4

Repeat Steps 2 and 3 to make a second two-patch square. Lay one square in front of you with the right side up. Take the second two-patch square, wrong side up, turn it 180 degrees and lay it down on top of the first square. The diagonal seams should be lying on top of one another, as should the contrasting colours. Align all four raw edges and pin or tack in place down one side, starting at a corner where the diagonal seams meet. Stitch a ⅜in (1cm) seam along this edge. Press open with a hot iron.

TIP

THE 'BIAS' IS WHERE THE WEAVE OF THE FABRIC RUNS DIAGONALLY TO THE HORIZONTAL AND VERTICAL GRAIN. FABRIC STRETCHES WHEN PULLED IN THIS DIRECTION AND CAN EASILY LOSE SHAPE WHILE YOU ARE PATCHING. RE-TRIMMING THE SQUARES IN STEPS 3 AND 7 HELPS TO CORRECT THIS.

Step 5

Make another identical four-patch piece. Lay one four-patch piece down in front of you, right side up. Take the second four-patch piece, turn it wrong side up, turn it 180 degrees and lay it down on top of the first square – the diagonal seams should be lying on top of one another, as should the contrasting colours. Align all four raw edges and pin or tack in place along the long edge where the diagonal seams all meet in the middle.

Step 6

Stitch a ⅜in (1cm) seam along this long edge. Press the seams open with a hot iron.

Step 7

Use template C on page 131 to square off the eight-patch square. Place it on top of the eight-patch piece, aligning its corners with the pressed diagonal seams at each corner. Draw around the square, and then trim the edges with sharp scissors to finish with a 9½in (24cm) square – use the red diagonal line on the template to help you do this.

Step 8

Repeat Steps 2–7 to make 16 eight-patch squares in total. Join these to make two strips of three squares and two strips of five squares.

Step 9

Lay out the plain linen and press. Mark a 27in (68cm) square in the centre of it, using a sharp pencil or an air-erasable pen. Take one of the strips of three eight-patch squares and lay it right side down so it is centred on the lining fabric and its long edge (furthest from you) butts up to the horizontal marked line furthest from you, 10½in (27cm) from the top raw edge. The body of the strip should fall towards the centre of the linen. Pin or tack along the top raw edge of the pieced strip.

Step 10

Stitch a ⅜in (1cm) seam along the top of the pieced strip. Remove the pins or tacking and fold the pieced strip up towards the top edge so that the raw edge is encased. Press with a hot iron. Pin and then tack the patched strip into position. The edge of the linen should extend several inches (centimetres) beyond the edge of the patched strip.

Step 11

Stitch the second short patched strip to the opposite end of your linen in the same way. Now take a long patched strip and lay it horizontally and right side down so that its left-hand edge butts up to the right-hand side of the marked line on the left of your linen and the top aligns with the top edge of one of the short strips. Pin or tack into position.

Step 12

Stitch the long strip down with a ⅜in (1cm) seam before folding the strip out, pressing and tacking down around its three raw edges.

Step 13

Press the front of your work with a hot iron and tack through the fabric layers all the way around the outside edge of the patchwork. Trim the linen flush with the edge of the patchwork border. Starting halfway along one side of your work, lay the bias binding and pin or tack it in position so that the middle of the binding lies exactly over the raw patched edge. Fold the starting edge of the binding forwards by ⅜in (1cm) and overlap this fold with ⅜in (1cm) of binding as you complete the circumference. Topstitch along the binding ⅛in (3mm) or less from the edge by machine.

Step 14

Create mitre folds at the corners to make them sharp and crisp. Take it slowly, following the instructions on page 121.

Step 15

With the wrong side of your work facing you, fold the binding over to encase the raw edges and hem by hand with overstitch.

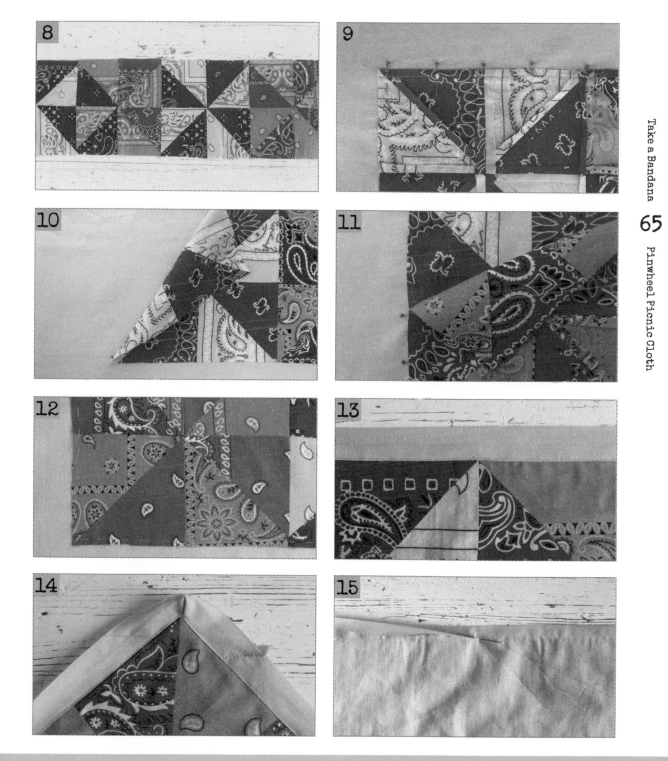

OUT AND ABOUT

This is a practical and reusable cover for a notebook or jotter. The elastic strap marks a page or keeps your book closed and your cuttings and receipts secure. It is a quick and easy project that would make a great gift.

NOTEBOOK COVER

Supplies:

To cover one notebook 6 x 8¼ x ½in (15 x 21 x 1.25cm):

☐ One 18in (46cm) square bandana, or fabric of your choice cut to those measurements

☐ 18 x 10in (46 x 25cm) of iron-on interfacing

☐ 10in (25cm) of elastic to match the colour of the bandana

☐ Scissors

☐ Iron

☐ Sewing machine

☐ Sewing needles and pins

☐ White cotton thread

☐ Thread to match the colour of the bandana

Step 1

Cut your bandana fabric to measure 18 x 10in (46 x 25cm). Fuse the iron-on interfacing to the wrong side of the bandana using an iron and following the manufacturer's instructions.

Step 2

Zigzag stitch around all four edges of your fabric and finish off the thread ends. With the wrong side facing, fold the two long edges over by $\frac{3}{8}$in (1cm) and stitch $\frac{1}{4}$in (5mm) from the zigzag edge to form a simple hem.

Step 3

Wrap the fabric (wrong side out) around the notebook, tucking the vertical, short edges inside the front and back covers. This allows you to make sure the pattern lies evenly along the vertical opening edges of the covers; ease the fabric back and forth until you are happy with the lie of the pattern over the book's front, spine and back. Mark the fabric at the top and bottom of the opening edges with pins through both layers of fabric to ascertain the position for the seams of the flaps.

Step 4

Slip the fabric off your notebook, retaining the pins in position. Fold back the right-hand flap enough to slip the length of elastic between the two layers of fabric and pin into position 2in (5cm) from the folded edge.

Step 5

Stitch $\frac{3}{4}$in (2cm) seams along the top edge, starting at one corner, then stitching across the two fabric layers of the flap, along the single layer between the two flaps and finally across the two layers of the other flap. Repeat along the bottom edge. Trim the four corners, turn right side out and press with an iron, folding the top and bottom edges between the flaps down along the stitch line.

TIP

YOU CAN CUSTOMIZE THE SIZE OF YOUR FABRIC NOTEBOOK COVER TO FIT DIFFERENT-SIZED NOTEBOOKS. CUT THE FABRIC TO MEASURE THE SAME HEIGHT AS THE NOTEBOOK PLUS $1\frac{1}{2}$IN (4CM) AND THE SAME WIDTH AS THE MEASUREMENT FROM THE RIGHT-HAND FRONT EDGE OF THE FRONT COVER, AROUND THE SPINE, AND TO THE LEFT-HAND EDGE OF THE BACK COVER PLUS $6\frac{1}{2}$IN (16CM).

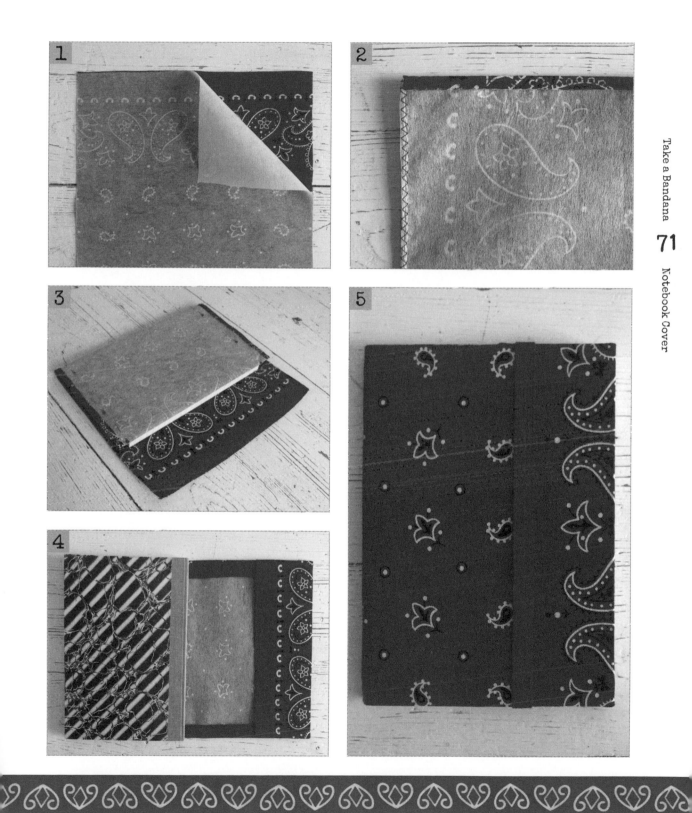

Make yourself a padded and quilted camera strap. Much more comfortable than a ready-made one, this brightly coloured strap has two little pockets for filters or a lens cap. Or, if you've returned to celluloid, you can keep spare rolls of film to hand.

CAMERA STRAP

Supplies:

- [ ] One bandana, minimum dimensions 20in (50cm) square, or fabric of your choice cut to those measurements
- [ ] 7 x 7½in (18 x 19cm) scrap of bandana or contrasting plain cotton for pocket linings
- [ ] 7 x 45in (18 x 115cm) of cotton wadding
- [ ] 7 x 45in (18 x 115cm) of fusible interfacing
- [ ] Scissors
- [ ] Sewing machine
- [ ] Thread to match the bandana
- [ ] Sewing needle and pins
- [ ] Iron

MEASURING THE STRAP

Measure the camera strap before cutting your fabric. The new strap needs to be about 2in (5cm) shorter than the existing one, so adjust your fabric, interfacing and wadding strip lengths accordingly, adding an extra ⅝in (1.5cm) in length to each strip for seam allowances. For the width, ensure an extra 1½in (4cm) to the widest part of your existing strap (this measurement includes a seam allowance).

Step 1

Cut the wadding and fusible interfacing into two long strips measuring 45 x 3½in (115 x 9cm). Cut 6in (15cm) from each strip of interfacing and wadding and put aside for the pockets. Shape both ends of the long strips of interfacing and wadding using the template on page 129. Cut five strips from the bandana, measuring 3½ x 20in (9 x 50cm). Cut two pieces from one of the strips of bandana to measure 3½ x 6½in (9 x 16cm) – these will be the pocket fronts. Now cut two pieces from the contrasting bandana or fabric to measure 3½ x 7½in (9 x 19cm) – these will be your pocket linings. Take four remaining bandana strips and shape one end of each using the template as a guide.

Step 2

Take two of the bandana strips, lay them right sides together and stitch a ⅜in (1cm) seam along the straight, unshaped short edges. Press open with a hot iron. Repeat with another pair. These will be the front and back of your strap.

Step 3

Take the strap front and lay it right side down in front of you. Fuse a strip of interfacing to it, centred on the fabric and thus leaving a ⅜in (1cm) seam allowance all the way around.

Step 4

Fuse a strip of wadding to the fabric, placing it directly over the interfacing. You may find it easier to fuse the wadding by turning your work over and ironing from the fabric side.

Step 5

Stitch a straight line down the centre of the long front and back pieces, and then three further lines ⅜in (1cm) apart to each side of the central line of stitching.

Step 6

Take one lining piece and fuse a rectangle of interfacing to it, and then a rectangle of wadding. Centre them across the width, but slightly off-centre across the length as shown. Leave ⅜in (1cm) at one end and ¾in (2cm) at the other end – this is the 'top' end.

Step 7

Lay this wadded lining piece on top of a pocket front, right sides together. Align the 'top' edge of the lining with one end of the pocket outer and pin or tack to hold in position.

Step 8

Stitch a seam ⅜in (1cm) from the top edge of the wadding and ⅜in (1cm) from the top raw edges. Press the seam open with a hot iron.

Step 9

Fold the pocket outer over along the top edge of the wadding. Align all the raw sides and bottom edges, thus creating a strip of lining to bind the top edge of your pocket. Press and pin or tack around the edges before topstitching just above the seam line at the top of the pocket.

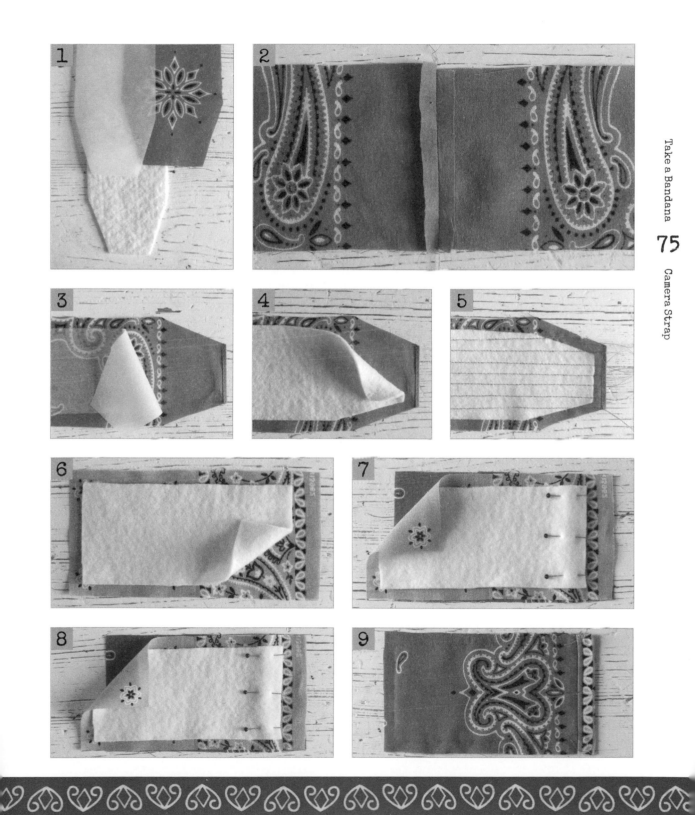

Step 10

Starting from the seam where the lining joins the pocket outer, mark and stitch a line down the centre of the pocket and three further lines ⅜in (1cm) apart to each side of the central line of stitching, just as you did with the front and back straps in Step 5. Start each line of stitching by lowering the needle into position by hand to ensure that it starts exactly on the seam line. Finish the thread ends at the top by hand with a sewing needle.

Step 11

With the pocket lining side up, fold the bottom edge over ¼in (5mm), press and stitch to make a small hem. Repeat Steps 6–11 to make the second pocket.

Step 12

To assemble your camera strap, take one pocket piece and lay it down lining side up. Place one end of your front piece over it so that the end of the strap front lies about ¼in (5mm) from the bottom edge of the pocket. Pin or tack in position. Do the same with the other pocket piece at the other end of this strip.

TIP

THIS PROJECT COULD ALSO BE MADE UP FROM LEFTOVER SCRAPS OF BANDANA. PIECE TOGETHER OFF-CUTS INTO LONG STRIPS, PRESSING THE SEAMS OPEN BEFORE CUTTING OUT THE TWO MAIN PATTERN PIECES AT STEP 1.

Step 13

Cut the corners off the pocket pieces flush with the end shaping of the strap piece. Fold both layers – pocket and front piece – over by ¼in (5mm). Press with an iron and stitch to form a hem, reverse stitching at either end. Take the strap lining strip and make a ¼in (5mm) hem on either short end in the same way. Turn the front/pocket strip over, right side up. Lay the lining strip on top of it, right side down. Align all edges and pin or tack.

Step 14

Leaving both short, hemmed ends open, sew a ⅜in (1cm) seam along both long edges, reverse stitching at the beginning and end for strength. The stitch line should fall just beyond the edge of the wadding. It may catch the wadding on the other side, but this isn't a problem. Finally, zigzag stitch along the raw edges of the two long seams to reduce fraying.

Step 15

Turn right side out through one of the short ends – take your time doing this, as it is slow work. Ease and manipulate the long seams to make them as sharp as possible and press with a hot iron. Unclip one end of the camera strap from your camera, feed it through the new strap and reattach it to your camera.

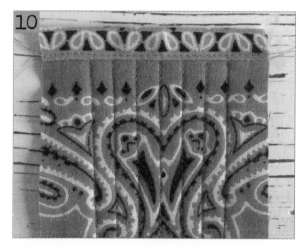

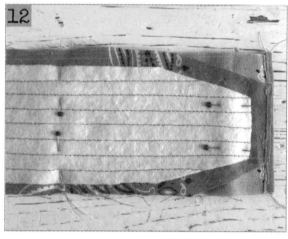

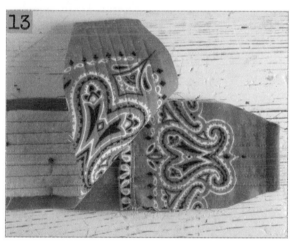

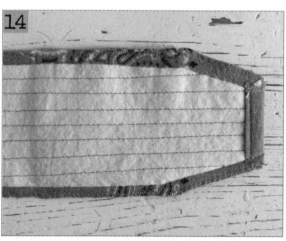

This is a quick project, ideal for using up scraps of bandana, that would make a perfect gift. It is a practical wallet for holding loyalty cards, travel cards, bankcards and receipts. Make it in monochrome or use up contrasting vibrant scraps.

FABRIC CARD HOLDER

Supplies:

- [ ] One bandana, minimum dimensions 18in (46cm) square, or scraps of different colours – see page 80 for dimensions needed
- [ ] 6 x 4½in (15 x 11.5cm) of heavyweight iron-on fabric stiffener
- [ ] 12in (30cm) square of iron-on interfacing
- [ ] 6in (15cm) of 1/16in (1mm)-wide cord elastic to match your bandana
- [ ] Scissors
- [ ] Iron
- [ ] Sewing machine
- [ ] Sewing needle and pins
- [ ] Threads to match your bandana

PREPARING THE PATTERN PIECES

From your bandana cut:

Outer: 6¾ x 5in (17 x 13cm)

Inside: 6¾ x 5in (17 x 13cm)

Tall pocket: 6¾ x 7½in (17 x 19cm)

Short pocket: 6¾ x 5½in (17 x 14cm)

From your interfacing, cut:

Tall pocket: 6 x 6¾in (15 x 17cm)

Short pocket: 6 x 4¾in (15 x 12cm)

Step 1

Using an iron, fuse the heavyweight stiffener to the centre of the wrong side of your outer piece, leaving ⅜in (1cm) all the way around. Fuse the interfacing to the centre of the wrong side of each pocket piece, leaving ⅜in (1cm) all the way around.

Step 2

Take the short pocket piece and fold it in half, wrong sides together, so that it now measures 6 x 2¾in (15 x 7cm) and press with an iron. Topstitch along the fold ⅛in (3mm) from the edge. Do the same with the tall pocket.

Step 3

Lay the lining piece down in front of you right side up. Place the tall pocket piece on top of it so that the raw edges along the bottom align with the raw edges of the bottom of the lining piece. Pin or tack along the bottom edge.

Step 4

Stitch a ¾in (2cm) seam along the bottom edge. Trim the seam to ¼in (5mm).

Step 5

Place the short pocket piece over the tall pocket and lining pieces so that its top edge lies 1in (2.5cm) below the top edge of the tall pocket and pin in position.

Step 6

Stitch along both side seams to hold the short pocket in position.

TIP

TAKE CARE WHEN USING IRON-ON STIFFENER OR INTERFACING. IT IS INCREDIBLY EASY TO PLACE THE WRONG WAY DOWN AND MAKE A MESS OF YOUR IRON. IDENTIFY WHICH SIDE HAS THE ADHESIVE ON IT: THIS CAN HAVE A BOBBLY, RAISED APPEARANCE AND A SLIGHT SHININESS FROM THE GLUE. THIS SIDE MUST ALWAYS BE FACE DOWN AND IN CONTACT WITH THE WRONG SIDE OF YOUR FABRIC.

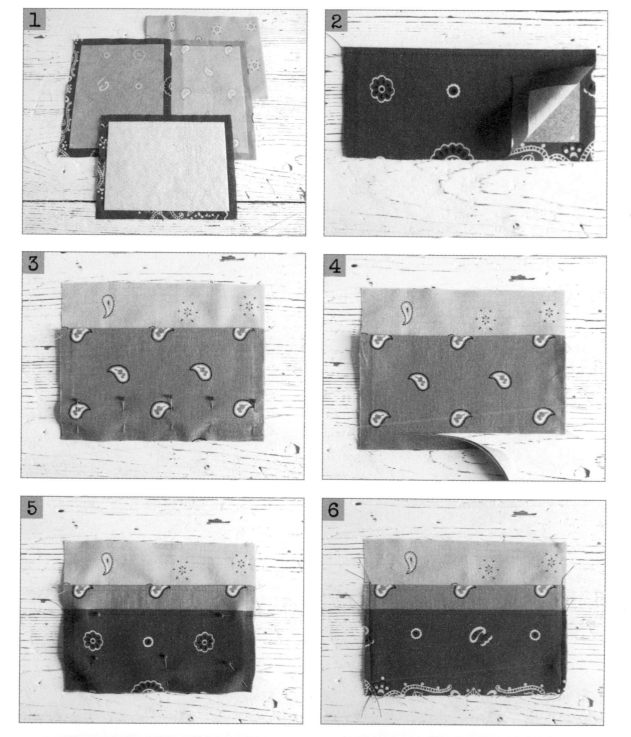

Step 7

Lay your outer piece down right side up. Fold your cord elastic in half and position halfway down the left-hand edge so that its raw ends are projecting just beyond the edge and the loop is lying horizontally across the centre of the fabric.

Step 8

Place the lining and pocket pieces right side down on top of the outer piece, aligning all the raw edges. The lining piece will be ¾in (2cm) shorter than the short pocket and the outer pieces at the bottom edge. Pin or tack in position.

Step 9

Sew a ⅜in (1cm) seam along both side edges and the top edge, then reverse stitch at the beginning and end for strength. Trim the seams down to ¼in (5mm). Clip the two top corners at 90 degrees.

Step 10

Slip your hand through the open bottom edge, in between the tall and short pocket layers, and turn the work out through this gap. Tease the seams and prod the top two corners from inside to make them sharp before pressing your work with an iron. Pin or tack along the raw bottom edge.

Step 11

Stitch a ⅜in (1cm) hem along the bottom edge, reversing at each end. Clip the two bottom corners, then turn out through the short pocket opening, prodding the two bottom corners from inside the short pocket to make them sharp. Press with a hot iron (avoid ironing the elastic).

Step 12

Topstitch just inside all four edges. 'Score' a vertical line up the centre of the pockets – I do this by running the tip of a small knitting needle, or a large tapestry needle, along the edge of a ruler. Stitch along the scored line by machine and finish off all thread ends carefully using a sewing needle.

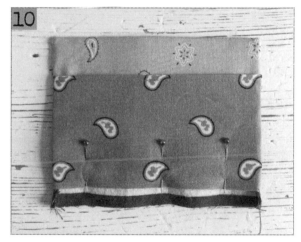

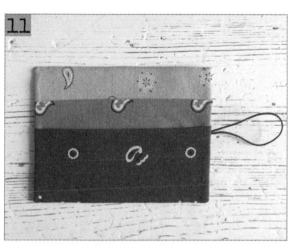

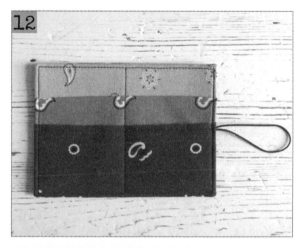

This is a neat little set of detachable pockets to keep essentials from disappearing into the depths of your bag. Attach this to the handles of your market basket and avoid scrabbling through your groceries for your keys or phone.

SHOPPING-BAG TIDY

Supplies:

- [ ] One bandana measuring 18in (46cm) square, or fabric of your choice cut to those measurements
- [ ] 10 x 7in (25 x 18cm) of cotton wadding
- [ ] 10 x 7in (25 x 18cm) of fusible interfacing
- [ ] 10 x 7½in (25 x 19cm) of heavyweight iron-on fabric stiffener
- [ ] 10½ x 12in (27 x 30cm) of linen for backing and binding
- [ ] Two self-cover buttons ¾in (2cm) in diameter
- [ ] 24in (60cm) of ⅛in (3mm)-wide cord elastic
- [ ] Two small buttons
- [ ] Scissors
- [ ] Iron
- [ ] Sewing needles and pins
- [ ] White cotton thread
- [ ] Thread to match the base colour of your bandana
- [ ] Sewing machine

Step 1

Cut two rectangles from the bandana: 10 x 8in (25 x 20cm) and 10 x 7in (25 x 18cm). Using an iron, fuse the cotton wadding to the wrong side of the smaller piece of bandana fabric with the fusible interfacing. Fuse the heavyweight fabric stiffener to the wrong side of the larger piece of bandana fabric, starting ⅜in (1cm) below the top edge.

Step 2

To make the back piece: lay the larger piece of bandana fabric down right side up in front of you and with the ⅜in (1cm) unstiffened edge furthest from you. Cut the elastic into two equal lengths and fold them in half. Pin each loop in position along the top edge, 2½in (6cm) from either end, with their raw edges just protruding over the top edge of the fabric.

Step 3

Lay the lining fabric on top, covering the elastic loops, aligning all edges and pinning or tacking along the top edge.

Step 4

Stitch a ⅜in (1cm) seam along the top edge, sewing through the two layers of fabric just outside the edge of the stiffener. Stitch back and forth as you pass over the ends of the elastic for extra strength. Open out and press the seam towards the bandana fabric, avoiding ironing the cord elastic.

Step 5

Fold the lining down behind, align all edges and press again. Pin or tack along all the sides and topstitch by machine ⅛in (3mm) in from the edges.

Step 6

To make the pocket: fold the padded piece of bandana fabric in half, wrong sides together, so that it now measures 10 x 3½in (25 x 9cm) and tack along the folded edge.

Step 7

Topstitch along the fold by machine ⅛in (3mm) from the edge. Lay it on top of the back piece, aligning the bottom and side edges. Pin or tack in position.

Step 8

Mark two vertical lines from the bottom of the pocket to the top edge of the pocket, one 4¼in (10.5cm) from the right-hand edge and one 2½in (6cm) from the right-hand edge. Stitch the two lines by machine, reversing at the top edge for extra strength.

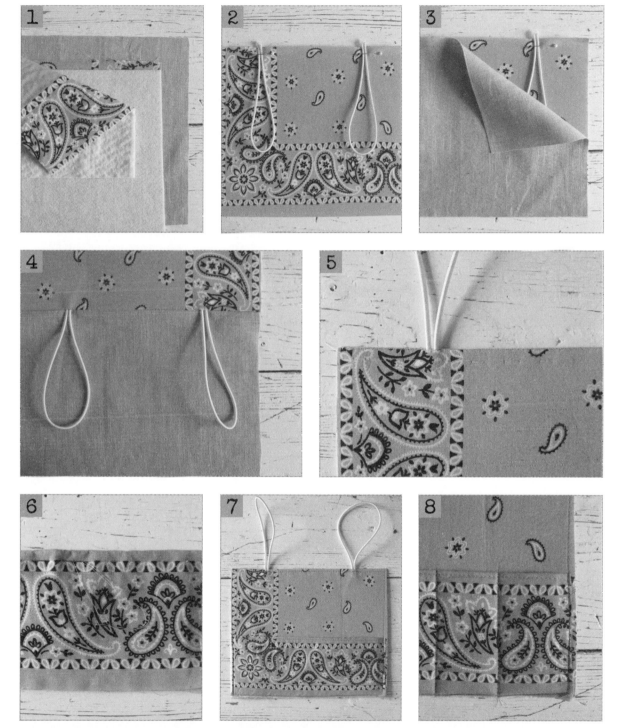

Step 9

Cut a strip of linen 10 x 1⅜in (25 x 3.5cm). Lay it face down along the bottom of the pocket, with the raw edges aligning. Pin or tack in position before stitching a ¼in (5mm) seam using thread to match the colour of the linen.

Step 10

Trim the selvedge down to make it even and fold the edge of the linen over twice to cover the raw edge of the seam and meet the stitch line on the back of your work. Pin or tack and hem by hand using overstitch.

Step 11

Turn your work back over (bandana side up). Cut two more strips of linen, 8¾ x 1⅜in (22 x 3.5cm). Take one and pin it along the right-hand edge of your work, aligning the raw edges and leaving the ends to overhang by ⅜in (1cm) at the top and bottom. Pin or tack into position before stitching a ¼in (5mm) seam using thread to match the colour of the linen.

TIP

YOU COULD USE UP SCRAPS FROM OTHER PROJECTS TO MAKE THIS. CUT PAPER PATTERNS FIRST TO ALL THE CORRECT DIMENSIONS TO WORK OUT IF YOU HAVE LARGE ENOUGH PIECES TO USE.

Step 12

Trim the selvedge down to make it even and fold the edge of the linen over twice to cover the raw edge of the seam and meet the stitch line on the back of your work. Pin or tack and hem by hand using overstitch. As you do so, fold in ⅜in (1cm) at the top and bottom to cover any raw edges and make neat corners. Repeat this process with the other strip of linen along the left-hand edge.

Step 13

Turn your work right side up. Stitch the two small buttons at the top of either vertical line of pocket stitching using thread to match the bandana.

Step 14

Use scraps of your bandana fabric to cover the two self-cover buttons following the instructions on page 125. Stitch them into position, each one ¾in (2cm) below the two loops of elastic, as shown.

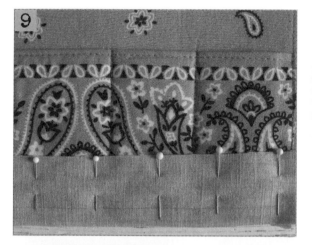

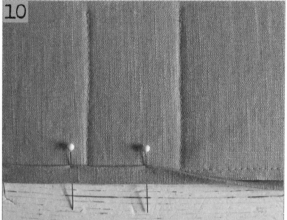

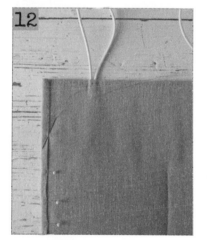

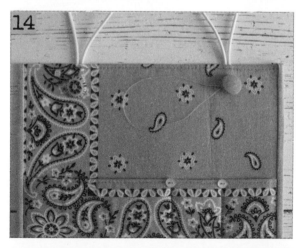

TIP

THIS PROJECT CAN BE MADE TO
MANY DIFFERENT DIMENSIONS,
JUST ADAPT IT TO SUIT YOUR NEEDS.
DIFFERENT-SIZED POCKETS AND
EVEN A LITTLE ZIPPED PURSE,
COULD BE INCORPORATED.

THE BEDROOM

This simple nightdress or lingerie case slips neatly under your pillow, is useful for travelling or to keep laundry separate in your suitcase. Resize the depth to 12in (30cm) plus a 6in (15cm) flap if you want to make a bigger one to fit pyjamas by using two bandanas.

NIGHTDRESS CASE

Supplies:

- [ ] One bandana, minimum measurement 22in (56cm) square, or fabric of your choice cut to those measurements
- [ ] 15 x 21½in (38 x 55cm) of white cotton or linen for lining
- [ ] 15 x 21½in (38 x 55cm) of fusible interfacing
- [ ] Three small buttons
- [ ] One Dorset button, ¾in (2cm) in diameter (see page 124 for making instructions)
- [ ] White crochet thread or cotton embroidery thread
- [ ] Scissors
- [ ] Iron
- [ ] Sewing needles and pins
- [ ] White cotton thread
- [ ] Thread to match your bandana (just a small amount for attaching the buttons and topstitching)
- [ ] Sewing machine

Step 1

Cut off the seams and press the bandana with a hot iron. Trim the bandana, interfacing and lining to 13¾ x 19in (35 x 48.5cm) and use the iron to fuse the interfacing to the wrong side of the bandana. Keep the scraps for binding the sides of your case later. With the bandana right side up, lay the lining fabric on top of it and align all the raw edges.

Step 2

Pin or tack along the two short ends and stitch a ⅜in (1cm) seam.

Step 3

Turn right side out and tease the two seams so that the edges are sharp before pressing them. Pin or tack along these edges and topstitch ⅛in (3mm) from the pressed edges – I worked from the bandana side and used white thread in the bobbin, with a thread matching the bandana on top.

Step 4

With your work wrong side up and lying vertically in front of you, fold the bottom edge up 7½in (19cm), press it, and pin or tack in position. Cut two strips from the bandana scraps to measure 1½ x 14¼in (4 x 36cm) for binding the two sides of your case. Lay your work bandana side up, pin one of the long strips along one of the long raw edges, right sides together. Position so that it extends about ⅜in (1cm) at either end, trimming it to this measurement if necessary. Pin or tack in position.

Step 5

Stitch a ⅜in (1cm) seam along this edge. Fold up the binding to cover the seam selvedge and press. Turn your work over, fold the top edge of the binding strip down to meet the raw edge of the seam, and press. Finally, fold the binding down again to meet the stitch line of the seam and pin or tack in position.

Step 6

Folding the extra binding in at either end, sew the binding down by hand with a small overstitch.

Step 7

Make the ¾in (2cm)-diameter Dorset button (see page 124). You can leave it plain, or embroider on it to mimic the motifs in the bandana, or maybe 'half-make' its centre so that it resembles a wagon wheel. Folding the flap of your case down 4½in (11.5cm), decide upon the position of the button and stitch it on so that it sits ¾in (2cm) below the edge of the folded-down flap. Sew on the button.

Step 8

To reduce the chance of the fabric tearing around the button, you can reinforce it by sewing a very small button onto the inside of the case, sandwiching the fabrics in between. Stitch two small buttons at the top left- and right-hand corners of the pocket to reinforce the stress point.

Step 9

Make a button loop (see page 126) to correspond with the Dorset buttons, either in white or to match the colour of your bandana.

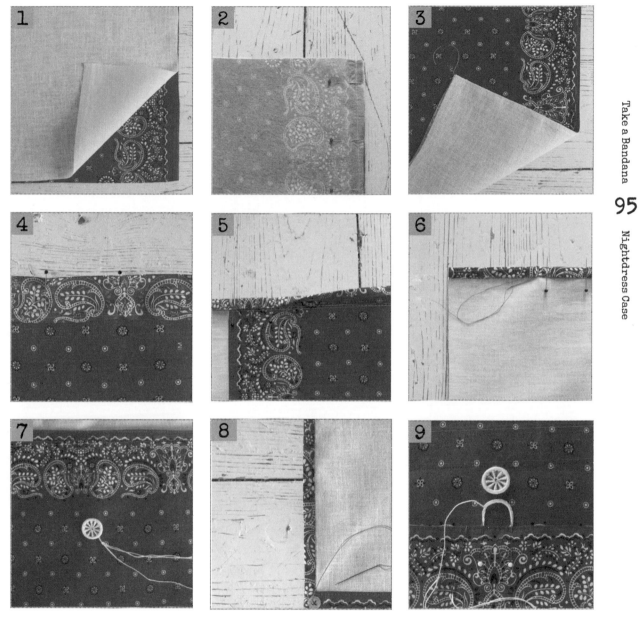

These are useful, simple bags for storing shoes, whether stashing them away when they're out of season, popping in a suitcase or keeping them in pairs at the bottom of your wardrobe. The size shown is designed for a pair of women's flat-heeled shoes.

SHOE BAGS

Supplies:

- [ ] One bandana, minimum measurement 20in (50cm) square, or fabric of your choice cut to those measurements
- [ ] 17 x 14in (43 x 35.5cm) of white cotton or linen for lining
- [ ] 28in (70cm) of ⅜in (1cm)-wide white herringbone tape for drawstring
- [ ] One small button
- [ ] Scissors

- [ ] Sewing needles and pins
- [ ] White cotton thread
- [ ] Sewing machine
- [ ] Iron
- [ ] Safety pin
- [ ] Thread to match your bandana (just a small amount for attaching the button)
- [ ] Sewing machine

Step 1

Trim the bandana so that it measures 20in (50cm) square. Lay the lining fabric down vertically in front of you. Lay the bandana right side down on top of it and align all the raw edges. Pin or tack along the top edge and stitch a ⅜in (1cm) seam.

Step 2

Press the seam towards the lining side. With the fabric laid out right side up and horizontally in front of you, fold the bottom long edge up to meet the top long edge. Carefully pin or tack all the way along this top edge, making sure that the seam is well aligned. Mark a ¾in (2cm) gap for the drawstring, starting 5½in (14cm) before and finishing 6in (15cm) before the bandana meets the lining. Stitch a ⅜in (1cm) seam along this long edge.

Step 3

Press the long seam open. Turn open the raw edges of the selvedge around the opening gap and stitch down by hand to reduce fraying.

Step 4

With your long tube of fabric still inside out, press it flat so that the long seam lies centrally along its length. Align the fabric at the lining end and pin or tack. Stitch a ⅜in (1cm) seam along the edge, leaving a 5in (13cm) turning gap. Trim the two corners at 45 degrees to make them nice and sharp when you turn the bag out.

Step 5

Align the fabric at the bandana end and pin or tack. Stitch a ⅜in (1cm) seam along this edge. If it is fairly fine fabric it is not necessary to trim the corners at 45 degrees.

Step 6

Pull your bag right side out gently through the turning gap.

Step 7

At the lining end, fold in the raw edges of the turning gap by ⅜in (1cm) and pin. Close the gap by hand with small overstitches.

Step 8

Push the bandana outer down inside the lining so that the corners meet snugly. In doing so, the bandana fabric folds over to line the top 3¼in (8cm) of your bag. Check on the bandana side that the drawstring gap is positioned just below the bandana/lining seam. Press with a hot iron and pin or tack along the seam joining the two fabrics. Sew two lines of stitching, one just below the seam on the lining, and the other ⅝in (1.5cm) below it to create a channel for the drawstring. Finish the thread ends off neatly by hand.

Step 9

Take the length of herringbone tape and feed it through the drawstring channel using a safety pin.

Step 10

Fold both ends of the tape over by ¼in (5mm) and then ¼in (5mm) again. Stitch them down securely by hand. Make sure that the protruding herringbone-tape tail ends are the same length. Find the centre of the back of your bag and stitch a small button through both layers of fabric and the tape to anchor it firmly in place – this will prevent the tape ends from disappearing into the channel in the future.

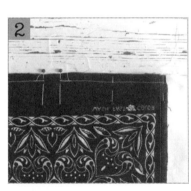

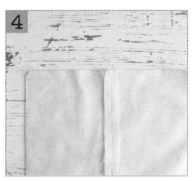

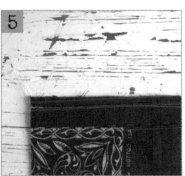

TIP

TO MAKE BAGS FOR BULKY SHOES, FIRST WRAP THEM WITH PAPER AND THEN USE THE SIZE OF THE PAPER AS YOUR PATTERN. ADD 6½IN (16CM) TO THE WIDTH AND 13IN (33CM) TO THE LENGTH. MAKE THE OUTER FABRIC 7IN (18CM) LONGER THAN THE LINING FABRIC. FOR MUCH LARGER BAGS, PIECE MORE THAN ONE BANDANA TOGETHER.

These nostalgic padded coat hangers are kind to your clothes, with the benefit of being 'non-slip' for finer garments. A nice touch for a guest room or a thoughtful present, this is a quick project with very satisfying results – you won't stop at making one.

COVERED COAT HANGER

Supplies:

For each coat hanger:

- [ ] One bandana, a minimum of 18in (46cm) square, or fabric of your choice cut to this measurement
- [ ] 4in (10cm) square scrap of bandana
- [ ] 70 x 1½in (180 x 4cm) of cotton wadding (this can be made out of several strips sewn together by hand)
- [ ] One small button
- [ ] Staple gun (optional)

- [ ] Scissors
- [ ] Sewing needle, thread and pins
- [ ] Sewing machine
- [ ] Iron
- [ ] Embroidery thread to match (or contrast) with your fabric
- [ ] Embroidery needle
- [ ] Yo-yo maker (optional)

Step 1

Wrap the strip of wadding around the hanger, overlapping it as you go. Stitch the end down by hand to anchor it, or use a staple gun to attach the wadding at the end of each arm of the hanger.

Step 2

Cut two pieces of bandana 15 x 5in (38 x 13cm). Place the two pieces of fabric right sides together and pin or tack along one short edge before machine stitching a $\frac{3}{8}$in (1cm) seam. Press the seam open with a hot iron.

Step 3

Turn the fabric over (now right side up and lying horizontally in front of you), fold the long bottom edge up to meet the top edge, and pin around the three raw edges.

Step 4

Rounding off the corners, stitch a $\frac{3}{8}$in (1cm) seam by machine, starting at the centre top (reverse stitching here for strength) and around one end, to meet the fold on the bottom edge. Stitch a similar seam on the other end, but this time starting 4in (10cm) from the end, thus leaving a large turning gap of roughly 9in (23cm) along one side of the top edge.

Step 5

Turn right side out through the turning gap. Turn in the raw edges of the gap by $\frac{3}{8}$in (1cm), press, and tack around the opening. At this point you may want to check whether the opening is big enough to slot your hanger into.

Step 6

Starting at the top centre, working away from the turning gap and using your embroidery thread, sew running stitches by hand approximately $\frac{1}{8}$in (3mm) around the fabric until you reach the other side of the turning gap. With the needle and thread still attached, feed your coat hanger into the fabric 'tube'. Pull your embroidery thread and tease the fabric so that it is gathered evenly across the width of the hanger.

Step 7

With the two tacked and folded edges held together, carry on with your running stitch to close the turning gap. Finish the embroidery thread off with a few tight, small stitches.

Step 8

Make $1\frac{3}{4}$in (4.5cm) yo-yos to stitch onto your padded coat hanger. You can use a yo-yo maker, in which case simply follow the manufacturer's instructions, or follow the instructions on page 127.

TIP

ALL INSTRUCTIONS ARE TO FIT A STANDARD SIMPLE $16\frac{1}{2}$IN (42CM)-WIDE CRESCENT-SHAPED WOODEN COAT HANGER.

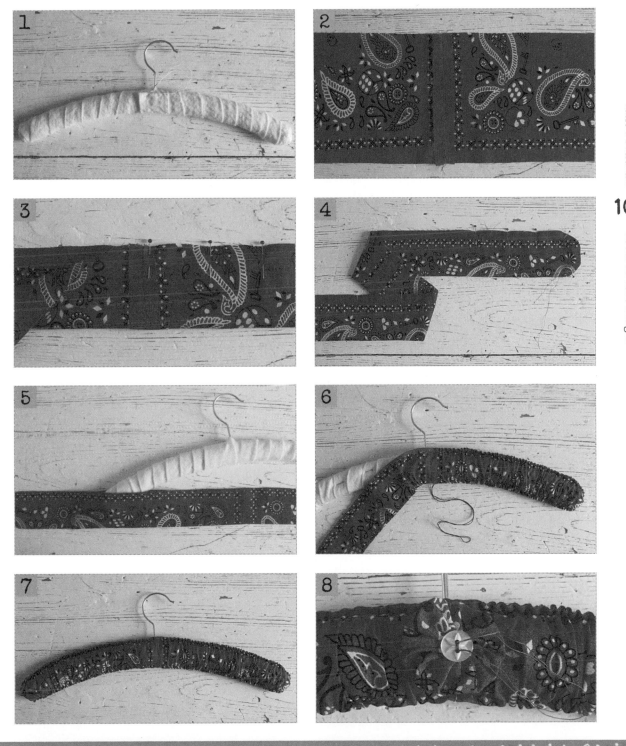

A classic red and white quilt made with nine bandanas. Each bandana becomes unique when juxtaposed with the others and their apparent similarities disappear. A cotton-filled quilt is cool to sleep under in the summer and a cosy extra layer as the nights draw in.

QUILT

Supplies:

- ☐ Nine bandanas, each 20in (50cm) square, or fabric of your choice cut to those measurements (I used simple, bold red bandanas, but any colour, or a mixture of many colours, would work well)
- ☐ 120in (3m) of white cotton, 44in (112cm) wide, for banding and borders
- ☐ 165in (4.2m) cotton, 44in (112cm) wide, for backing

- ☐ 82in (206cm) square of natural cotton wadding
- ☐ Iron
- ☐ Measuring tape
- ☐ Scissors
- ☐ Sewing needles and pins
- ☐ Sewing machine
- ☐ White cotton thread
- ☐ Quilting thread (if quilting by hand)

PREPARE THE BANDANAS

Iron the bandanas and measure them to find the shortest dimension of all of them. My shortest dimension was 19¼in (49cm), so all the calculations and measurements here are based on the bandanas being trimmed to the same size, i.e. 19¼in (49cm) squares. Cut the smallest bandana square: take its shortest side and cut the others to match this measurement. You should now have a perfect square, even if the pattern on it is a bit askew. Cut the other eight bandanas to match the size of the first. Arrange the bandanas into a three-by-three grid to decide on their positions. Take a photo once you've decided on the layout so that you can refer to it as you piece the bandanas together. Alternatively, sketch a nine-square grid and number the squares 1–9. Pin numbered pieces of paper onto the bandanas reflecting their grid position.

PREPARE THE WHITE BANDING AND BORDER FABRIC

Cut the white cotton along its length to make:
12 strips of fabric 4¼ x 19¼in (10.5 x 49cm) = **A**
4 squares of fabric 4¼ x 4¼in (10.5 x 10.5cm) = **B**
2 strips of fabric 63 x 10in (160 x 25cm) = **C**
2 strips of fabric 81½ x 10in (207 x 25cm) = **D**
(Cut strips **C** and **D** first)
You now need to start joining the bandanas to the white 'banding' in strips.

Step 1

Take bandana 1 (top left of the grid) and a short strip of fabric (**A**). With the bandana right side up, place the white strip on top of it, along its right-hand side. Align the raw edges and pin or tack.

Step 2

Stitch a ⅜in (1cm) seam. Open out and press.

Step 3

Join bandana 2 (positioned top middle of the grid) to the **A** strip joined to bandana 1 in the same way. Take another strip **A** and join to the right-hand side of bandana 2. Finally, join bandana 3 (top right of the grid) to the **A** strip joined to bandana 2.

Step 4

Repeat this process with the second and third row of the grid to end up with three rows of bandanas, each made up of three bandanas separated by white **A** strips. Now make two long-pieced sections to join the three rows. These will BOTH be made up from joining the remaining strips thus: **A** + **B** + **A** + **B** + **A**. Press all the work.

Step 5

Lay down the top strip of the grid right side up. Place one of the pieced sections from step 4 right side down along the bottom edge of the row. Align the edges and seams before pinning or tacking.

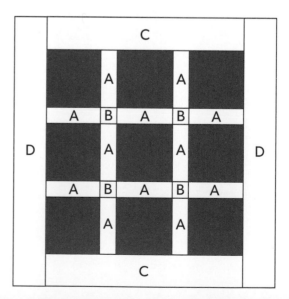

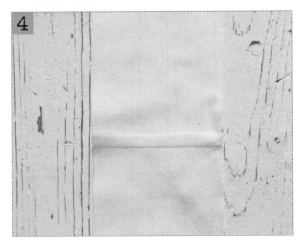

TIP

MAKE THIS QUILT LARGER OR
SMALLER BY SIMPLY ALTERING
THE NUMBER OF BANDANAS YOU
USE. MAKE UP THE FRONT PATCHED
PANEL FIRST SO THAT YOU CAN THEN
WORK OUT HOW MUCH WADDING AND
BACKING FABRIC YOU WILL NEED.

Step 6

Stitch a ⅜in (1cm) seam along this edge. Open out and press. With the work right side up, place the next row of joined bandanas face down along the bottom edge of the white pieced section. Align the edges and seams before pinning or tacking and stitching a ⅜in (1cm) seam. Open out and press with a hot iron. Continue this process with the remaining pieced section and the final row of joined bandanas. Press the work before joining the two **C** pieces followed by the two **D** pieces to frame the nine bandanas, pressing the work as you go. You have now completed the front of your quilt.

Step 7

Take the backing fabric and cut it in half. Join the two halves together to make a large square. If you have a large or geometric print (as I did here), use a hot iron to fold one selvedge edge under by ⅜in (1cm) or so. Lay it against the selvedge edge of the other half of the fabric and move it up and down, left and right, until you are happy with the pattern match. Pin or tack in position before topstitching ⅛in (3mm) from the folded edge to join the two pieces.

Step 8

Now lay the backing fabric right side down on a large table or the floor. Centre the wadding on top of it and then lay the pieced quilt front over them right side up.

Step 9

Starting at the centre of the patchwork, make long lines of tacking out to the edges, radiating from the centre to anchor the three layers together.

Step 10

Quilt by machine or by hand. Your stitching can follow a grid pattern, the designs in the bandanas themselves, or random paisley or floral shapes reflecting those used in traditional bandana designs – just experiment. Remove the tacking lines.

Step 11

Finish the quilt by binding the edges using 2in (5cm)-wide strips of fabric and mitred corners (see page 121). You will first need to trim your work all the way around – the fabric and wadding shift during the quilting process, leaving uneven edges. Join the 2in (5cm)-wide strips of fabric with short ⅜in (1cm) seams and press open. You will need enough to go all around your quilt, plus an extra 12in (30cm) to leave enough for the corners and finishing the ends with a neat overlap.

TIP

IF YOU ARE NOT CONFIDENT ENOUGH TO QUILT YOURSELF, MAKE ENQUIRIES AT A PATCHWORK SHOP OR LOOK ONLINE TO FIND A QUILTING SPECIALIST. IF YOU QUILT BY HAND, USE SMALL RUNNING STITCHES WORKING FROM THE CENTRE OUTWARDS TO AVOID TOO MANY WRINKLES AND PUCKERS. THERE ARE NUMEROUS BOOKS OR TUTORIALS ONLINE TO SUPPORT YOU.

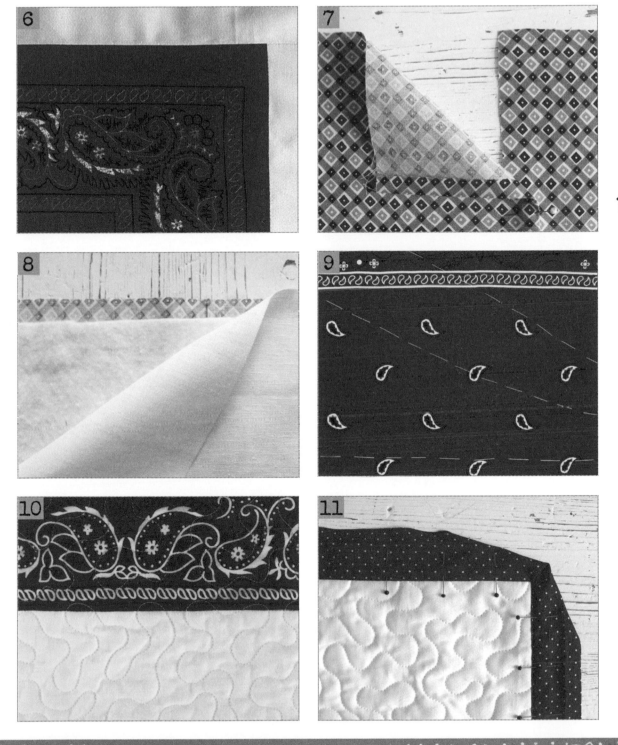

TECHNIQUES

MATERIALS AND EQUIPMENT

A sewing machine (see page 115) is essential for making the projects in this book. You will also need a steam iron and ironing board on hand to press your work as you go.

Other items you will need include: cotton bandanas (1), piping cord (2), cord elastic (3), pencil (4), air-erasable pen (5), threads (6), toggles (7), purse frame (8), buttons (9), measuring tape (10), self-cover buttons (11), ruler (12), herringbone tapes (13), embroidery threads (14), wooden bag handles (15), embroidery hoop (16), embroidery needles (17), pins (18), small brass curtain rings (19), yo-yo maker (20), bias binding (21), scissors (22), insulated wadding (23), fusible interfacing (24), cotton wadding (25), iron-on stiffener (26) and zipper sewing machine foot.

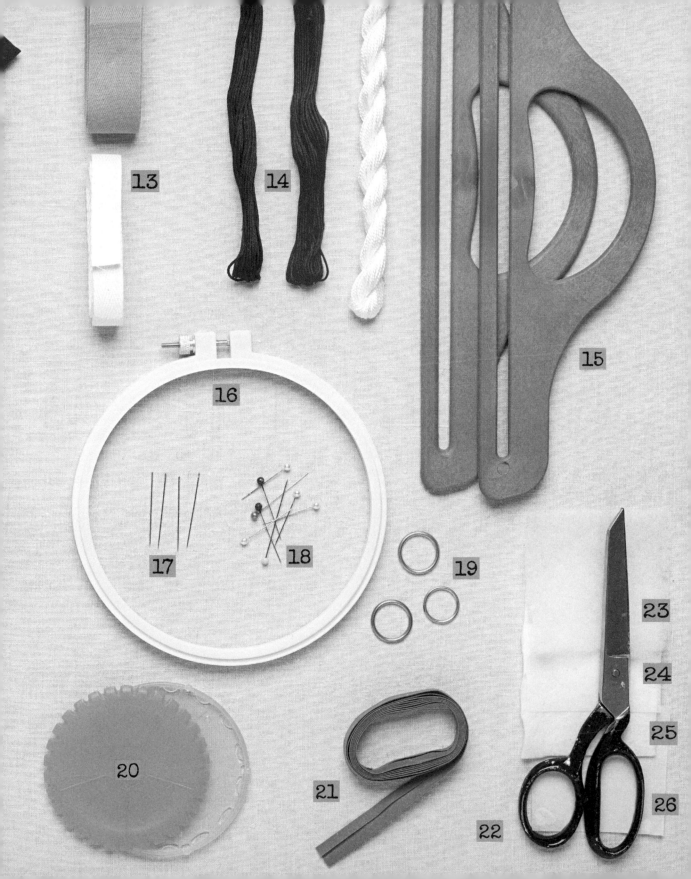

WORKING WITH FABRIC

CHOOSING FABRIC

Select natural fibres whenever possible: linens, cottons or linen/cotton mixes. Natural fibres are best washed before use to pre-shrink them. Choose good-quality stiffeners and interfacings. I always use natural cotton wadding.

For trims and ties, use traditional rickrack, piping cord, herringbone and woven tapes, 100% cotton threads and plain buttons – cover your own (see page 125) or make Dorset buttons (see page 124).

PATTERN PLACEMENT

If you are using a printed bandana for your project, it is worth spending time planning the placement of the design when cutting your fabric. The best way to do this is to cut a 'window' template. Cut your template shape out of the middle of a piece of paper and move it about over the fabric to choose the pattern section you like.

MEASURING

A measuring tape can be substituted with a ruler. Make sure you consistently use either imperial or metric measurements and do not mix the two.

MARKING

Use an air-erasable pen or a fabric marker. Most fade after a couple of hours, but do check as some need washing out. Tailor's chalk can be brushed away. Use white chalk on dark cloth and coloured chalk on lighter fabrics. The chalk should be kept sharp to produce a clean line. If your design is going to be stitched with a dark thread, you can simply use a very fine, sharp pencil to mark the fabric.

CUTTING

Ideally, you should have two pairs of sewing scissors. A small pair of sharp, pointed scissors is essential for cutting threads and trimming corners and curves. Sewing shears have long blades and a bent handle so that the scissors can rest on the table while cutting, keeping the fabric flat. Make sure your shears are used solely for fabrics and keep them sharp – it is a good idea to get them sharpened every couple of years.

PINNING AND TACKING (BASTING)

Pinning and tacking seams before you sew ensures that the fabric will not slip about when stitching, thereby producing a straight, neat seam. Pins with coloured glass heads are easy to find in fabric. Place your pins at right angles to your stitching line if you want to machine stitch over them and avoid having to tack or baste.

Tacking, also known as basting, is a temporary stitch used to fix pieces of fabric in position ready for permanent stitching. It is the easiest and quickest hand-sewing stitch. Knot the end of the thread and work large running stitches about ⅜in (1cm) long (**A**). Finish with a couple of stitches worked over each other to secure the end. When the seam or hem has been permanently sewn by machine, remove the tacking.

USING A SEWING MACHINE

It is important to keep your sewing machine regularly serviced and covered when not in use. Always refer to your instruction booklet for information on threading, changing stitches, reversing and so on.

Set up your machine somewhere with plenty of light and where you can sit at the machine comfortably.

Before sewing, make sure that the machine is threaded correctly and that the threads from the needle and bobbin are placed away from you towards the back of the machine. Turn the wheel towards you so that the needle is in the work, preventing a tangle of threads as you start. Taking it slowly will help you control the machine and make problems with the tension or tangling threads less likely to arise.

TWO-COLOUR SEWING

I regularly sew with one colour threaded on the machine needle and a different colour in the bobbin below. This is useful when sewing together two different-coloured fabrics, making the stitching less visible on both sides. I keep little pill boxes of fully charged bobbins in all the colours I'll be using in projects (A), so that I can swap the bobbin over quickly when I need to.

When using this technique it is especially important that your stitch tension is even so that the alternative colours are not pulled through to show on the other side of your fabric.

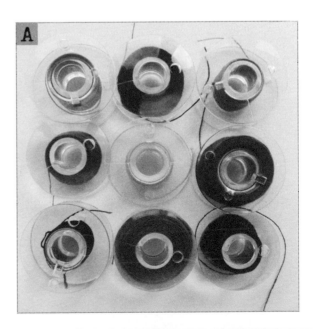

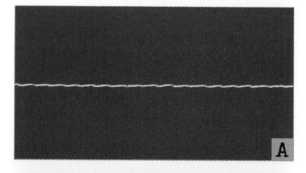

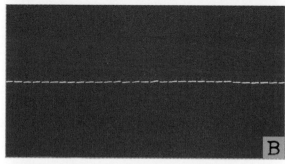

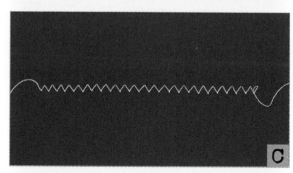

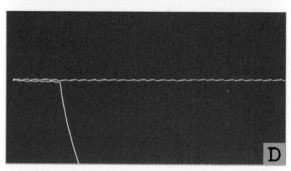

BASIC STITCHES

I don't go in for fancy sewing-machine stitching: the basics of straight stitching, zigzag stitching, topstitching and reverse stitching are all you need to make the projects in this book.

STRAIGHT STITCH (A)

Used for all flat seams, hems and topstitching. You can alter the length of straight stitch – at its longest it can be used for gathering or tacking (basting).

TOPSTITCHING (B)

A line of straight machine stitching worked on the right side of the fabric, parallel to seams and edges. It can be used as both a decorative and a functional stitch, providing extra strength to a hem or seam.

ZIGZAG STITCH (C)

Used along raw edges to help reduce fraying. Zigzag stitches can also be used decoratively or to strengthen pressure or stress points. You can alter the length of the stitches and how close together they are. When changing from straight stitch to zigzag (or vice versa) without breaking your stitching, always adjust your stitch function with the foot down (to hold your fabric in position) and the needle up.

REVERSE STITCHING (D)

This reinforces or strengthens the beginning and end of a line of stitching, particularly in areas where pressure or stress will occur. It can also be used as a quick way to start and end stitching without having to finish off thread ends by hand.

BASIC SEAMS

FLAT SEAMS (A)

Place the two pieces of fabric together, right sides facing. Pin or tack the fabric together. Machine stitch along your sewing line, ⅜in (1cm) from, and parallel to, the raw edges of the fabrics. Finish the beginning and end of your line of stitching either by hand or by reverse stitching.

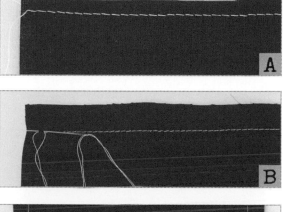

FINISHING OFF THREADS (B)

Finish off thread ends by threading them onto a sewing needle and either making a couple of small, tight stitches before cutting the thread off, or 'losing' the ends into a French seam or hem.

TRIMMING CORNERS AND CURVES (C)

Corners should be trimmed to an angle of 90 degrees so they are sharp when the work is turned right side out. On curved seams, cut V-shapes close to the stitch line. This will allow the seam to be smooth when the work is turned right side out.

PRESSING SEAMS (D)

Have all the equipment for ironing set up before you start a project. Press each seam as you complete it. Use the point of the iron to open seams, then steam press for a crisp edge and a flat seam.

UNPICKING SEAMS (E)

A seam ripper (or stitch unpicker) is a useful tool for unpicking stitches. Insert the pointed blade underneath the thread to be cut. Push it forwards against the thread and the blade will cut it. It is possible to run the blade along a line of stitching between the two layers of fabric and cut all the stitches in one movement, but this requires some skill to avoid cutting the fabric.

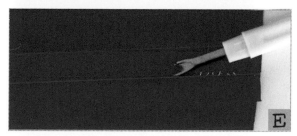

FLAT FELL SEAM

A flat fell seam is most commonly used on tailored shirts or the inside leg seam of jeans. It has one or two lines of visible stitching and no raw edges showing on either side. This seam is equally finished and neat on both sides and therefore perfect for use on reversible projects.

TIP

THESE SEAMS CAN BE FIDDLY TO DO AT FIRST. BE CAREFUL NOT TO SCORCH YOUR FINGERS AT STEP 3.

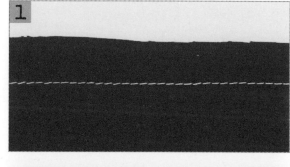

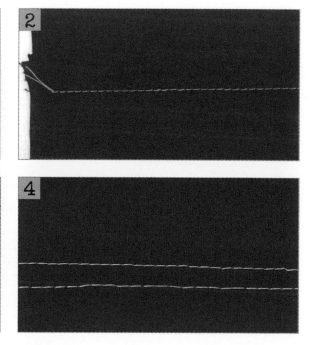

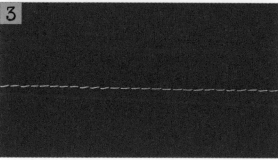

Step 1
To create a flat fell seam on the garment inside, stitch a ⅜in (1cm) seam with your fabrics wrong sides together.

Step 2
With the seam lying horizontal in front of you, press the seam away from you. Trim the front seam allowance to ⅛in (3mm) from the seam stitching.

Step 3
Fold the longer seam allowance over the trimmed portion and press in place. It is important that the fold width remains consistent along the seam. Press the whole of the folded seam allowance down towards you and pin or tack in position.

Step 4
Topstitch close to the folded edge to enclose the raw edges.

FRENCH SEAMS

Step 1
With the right sides of the fabric together, align the raw hem edges. Pin or tack together and stitch a ⅜in (1cm) seam along the edge.

Step 2
Trim the seam to ¼in (5mm).

Step 3
Turn the work wrong side out and press with an iron. Pin or tack all the way along the seam and stitch a ⅜in (1cm) hem, thus encasing the raw edges. Finally, turn right side out and press.

TIP

FRENCH SEAMS ARE AN EFFICIENT WAY TO PREVENT RAW EDGES FRAYING. THE SEAM COMPLETELY ENCASES THE EDGES, LEAVING A NEAT FINISH. THEY ARE IDEAL FOR ITEMS THAT MUST WITHSTAND A LOT OF WEAR.

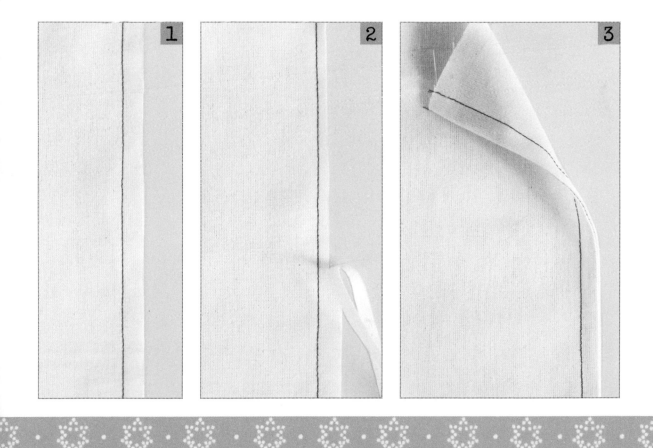

BINDING EDGES

Use tape, bias binding or strips of fabric to bind raw edges. If you are making your own binding from strips of fabric, cut them wider than needed, fold the long edges in and press them before starting.

Step 1

Cut the binding to the required length plus at least ¾in (2cm). Lay it along the edge of the work so that the middle lies exactly over the raw fabric edge. Pin or tack in position and topstitch along the binding ⅛in (3mm) or less from the edge. If binding all the way around a piece of work, join it by folding the end under ⅜in (1cm), overlapping the beginning of the binding and stitching along this fold.

Step 2

Turn the work over. Fold the tape down to meet the stitch line and encase the raw edges. Hem by hand by overstitching.

BINDING AROUND CURVES

Any curved edges require fabric cut on the bias to avoid excessive puckering. The easiest way to do this is to use pre-made bias binding.

Step 1

Open the binding out. Place it on your work right sides together and position the upper fold in the binding along your stitch line. Tack in place and machine slowly and carefully along the fold crease.

Step 2

Fold the binding over the raw edges of your work to the other side. Fold the binding under and hem by hand by overstitching. Press on both sides.

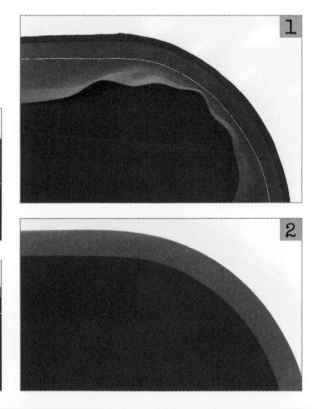

BINDING A MITRED CORNER

Mitred corners are crisp and sharp, and ideal for tablecloths and quilts. Use binding that measures twice the width you want it to finish up; so for a ½in (1.25cm) border use 1in (2.5cm)-wide binding.

Step 1

You need enough binding to cover the seams, plus 3in (7cm) for finishing off. Measure the width of the binding. Draw a line half the width of the binding in from the raw edges to be bound. Starting halfway along one edge, lay the binding right side up so that its bottom edge lies on your pencil line. Topstitch by machine very close to the bottom edge of the binding until you reach the corner turn of the pencil line. Remove your work from the machine and finish off the thread ends by hand.

Step 2

Fold the binding back under itself and upwards at 90 degrees.

Step 3

Now fold the binding back down under itself again 180 degrees so that the mitre's point lies exactly over the corner point of the fabric.

Step 4

Reinsert the machine needle where your last stitching finished, in the corner fold – turn the wheel by hand to place it accurately – and topstitch close to the edge of the binding along the edge of your work to the next corner.

Step 5

Turn the work over. Fold the binding down to encase the raw seam edge. Pin or tack in position before hemming all the way around by hand using overstitch. Take your time at the corners to fold neat mitres to mirror those on the other side.

Step 6

Press the binding from both sides.

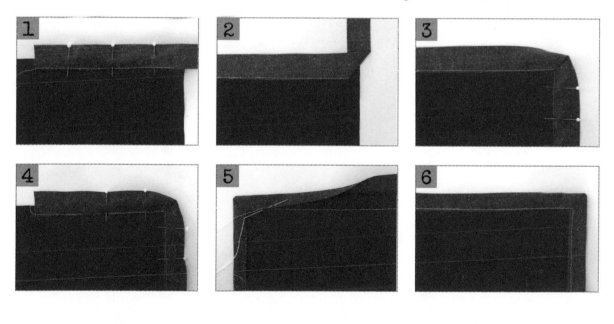

MAKING BOX CORNERS

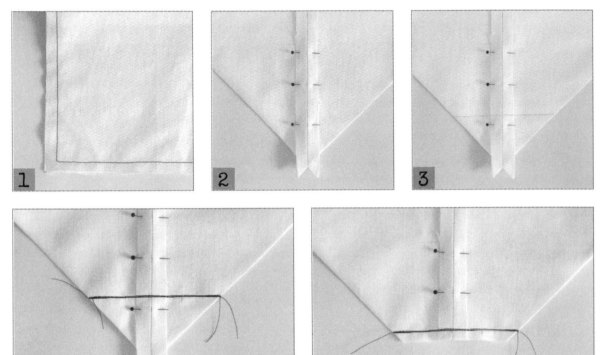

Step 1
Place the two pieces of fabric right sides together. Using a straight stitch, and the indicated seam allowance, sew the side and bottom seams. Pivot at the corners by leaving the needle down, raising the foot and turning the fabric 90 degrees.

Step 2
Press the seams open. With the sewn fabric still right sides together, match the side seam with the bottom fold (or seam) to create a point at the corner. Pin to hold them together. It is very important to match the seams exactly; this will make the finished corner look good.

Step 3
Mark the line of the box corner with a pencil so the depth is measured from side to side at the base of the point. This boxed corner depth is 4in (10cm), measured from the tip of the corner.

Step 4
Sew across the point on the drawn line several times, reverse stitching at the beginning and end for extra strength.

Step 5
Trim away the peak to ¼in (5mm) from the line.

HAND FINISHING STITCHES

OVERSTITCH (A)

Use overstitch for closing openings left for turning. With your two pieces of fabric pinned or tacked together, bring your needle up from within one folded edge to the front of your work. Now push the needle diagonally through both folded layers, catching a few threads of fabric from each.

Pull the needle and thread through and repeat, spacing the stitches between ⅛in (3mm) and ¼in (5mm) apart.

HEM STITCH (B)

Similar to overstitch, this stitch is used for hand stitching hems.

TIP

RUN THE NEEDLE ALONG THE INSIDE OF THE FABRIC FOLD BETWEEN STITCHES TO KEEP THE WORK ALMOST INVISIBLE.

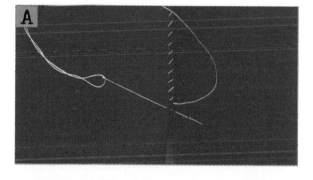

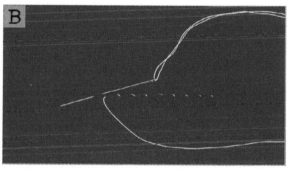

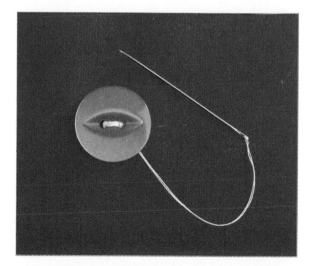

SEWING ON BUTTONS

Mark the position for your button on the fabric. With the thread doubled, tie a knot at the end and pull the needle through to the front of your fabric. Sew the button on securely through the holes, then pull the needle through between the button and the fabric. Wind the thread around the stitches connecting the button to the fabric twice. Insert the needle through to the back of the fabric and finish off with a couple of small, tight stitches.

DORSET BUTTONS

This style of button dates back to 1600. They add beautiful character to any hand-stitched project. It takes some practice to get the crossing of the 'spokes' central, so don't worry if your wheel is off-centre – this can be excused as handmade charm.

Step 1

Thread an embroidery needle with thread. Tie one end of the thread onto the curtain ring. Work in blanket stitch around the circumference of the ring, covering the raw knot end with the first few stitches.

Step 2

Make sure you make enough stitches to cover the ring completely. Stitch into the first stitch again to hide the join. Slide the stitches around the ring so that the outside blanket stitch ridge is now on the inside of the ring and the outside edge is completely smooth.

Step 3

Wrap your thread around the ring from top to bottom. Turn the ring slightly and wrap the thread around again. Continue until you have wrapped ten times to create the spokes of the wheel. At this point the threads will look somewhat random; use the end of your needle to tweak and reposition them so they are dispersed evenly around the ring. Make a couple of stitches in the centre of the wheel to secure the spokes and even them out.

Step 4

Using backstitch, work your way around the spokes in a clockwise spiral from the centre outwards. Thread ends can be finished off, but leave one or two of them long to fix your button to the fabric.

TIP

USE DIFFERENT-COLOURED THREADS IN STEPS 2, 3 AND 4 TO CREATE INTERESTING NEW DESIGNS FOR YOUR BUTTONS.

SELF-COVERED BUTTONS

A wonderful way to co-ordinate or contrast buttons is by covering them in fabric. Self-cover buttons have a front and a back piece, plus instructions for the amount of fabric needed for each button.

Step 1
Cut out a circle of fabric at least ⅜in (1cm) larger all the way around than the button front (check the manufacturer's instructions for exact sizing). For the Shopping-bag tidy (see page 84), you will need to cut out a circle of fabric 1½in (4cm) in diameter.

Step 2
With the fabric right side down, place the top part of the button centrally on top of it, with the open 'toothed' side facing you. Tuck the edges of the fabric in so that the 'teeth' of the button grip them and the fabric lies smoothly over the smooth surface of the button.

Step 3
Clip the two halves of the button together, using a small pair of pliers to make sure they are firmly connected if necessary.

Step 4
Turn the button over and press and smooth the edges to minimize any wrinkles or tucks.

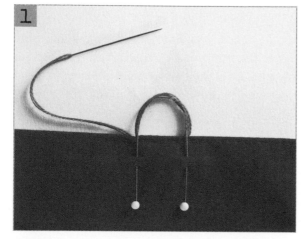

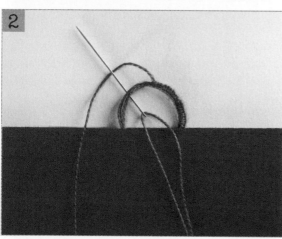

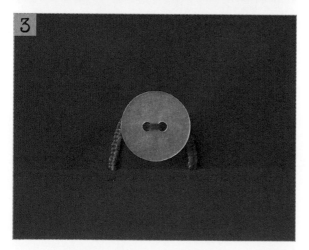

BUTTON LOOPS

Step 1

Sew on the button. Use pins to mark the position of the loop. Push the threaded needle up through the fabric's folded edge at the point of the left-hand pin, leaving the knotted end within the fold. Push the needle back in again at the point of the right-hand pin and out again by the left-hand pin. Pull the needle to leave a loop of thread wide enough to go over the button. Repeat stitching through at the two marker pins until the loop has four strands.

Step 2

Remove the two marker pins. Starting at the right-hand side, sew small buttonhole stiches (blanket stitches) over all the strands and the loose thread until you reach the left-hand side. Fasten off securely with a few small, tight stitches.

Step 3

You could play around with colours for the loop and the thread with which you stitch your button on.

TIP

THESE ARE MUCH EASIER TO MAKE FOR SMALL BUTTONS THAN TRADITIONAL BUTTONHOLES AND ARE VERY SATISFYING TO SEW.

MAKING A YO-YO

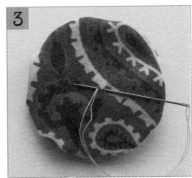

TIP

THESE EMBELLISHMENTS ARE PERFECT FOR USING UP SCRAPS TO DECORATE PROJECTS OR MAKE SWEET LITTLE CORSAGES WITH A BUTTON OR A BEAD IN THE CENTRE.

A yo-yo is used to embellish the Covered Coat Hanger (see page 100). If you have a yo-yo maker, simply follow the manufacturer's instructions. Otherwise follow the instructions below.

Step 1

Cut a circle of fabric 4in (10cm) in diameter. With the wrong side facing you, fold the edges in by ¼in (5mm) and press with a hot iron. With the wrong side still facing you, bring the needle through from the back and make ¼in (5mm) gathering stitches (like stitching a hem), all around the edge with your thread doubled for strength.

Step 2

Draw your thread to gather in the folded edge to the centre.

Step 3

Push the needle through the centre to the back and make a few small stitches to finish off the thread and firmly secure the gathering.

Step 4

When complete, stitch the yo-yo onto the project you have made. You can use a small button to anchor the yo-yo into position.

Templates

All the templates you need for the projects are found here. Remember, if you want to use pattern placement in your project by using the bandana border and central patterns strategically, cut these as 'window templates' (see page 114) and take your time to position them on your fabric before pinning and cutting.

Enlarge the templates on a photocopier set at 200%, printing onto A3 paper. Align each template as near to the top left-hand corner of the photocopier glass as possible. You may need to repeat this a few times, tweaking the position on the glass as needed to make the whole template fit onto the paper. Now they are ready to cut out and use.

Patchwork pincushion (see page 28)
Copy at 200%

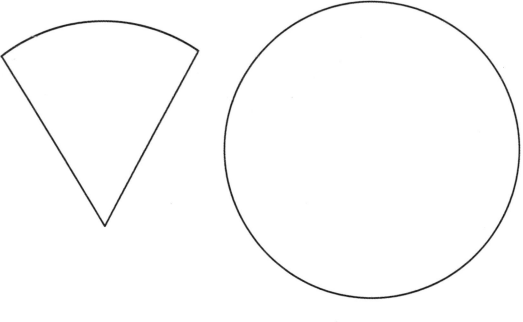

Pincushion front segment

Cut 6 in bandana fabric
(includes seam allowance)

Pincushion back

Cut 1 in backing fabric
(includes seam allowance)

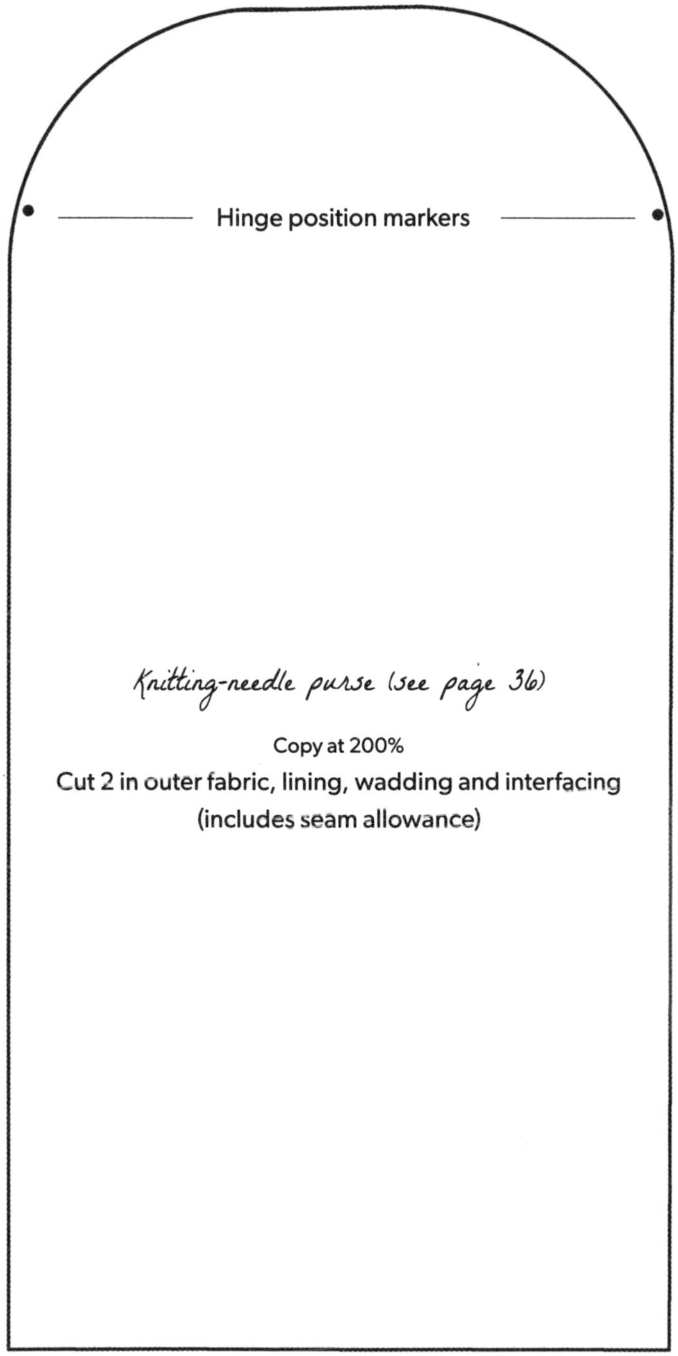

Hinge position markers

Knitting-needle purse (see page 36)

Copy at 200%
Cut 2 in outer fabric, lining, wadding and interfacing
(includes seam allowance)

Camera strap (see page 72)
Shaped end template
Copy at 200%

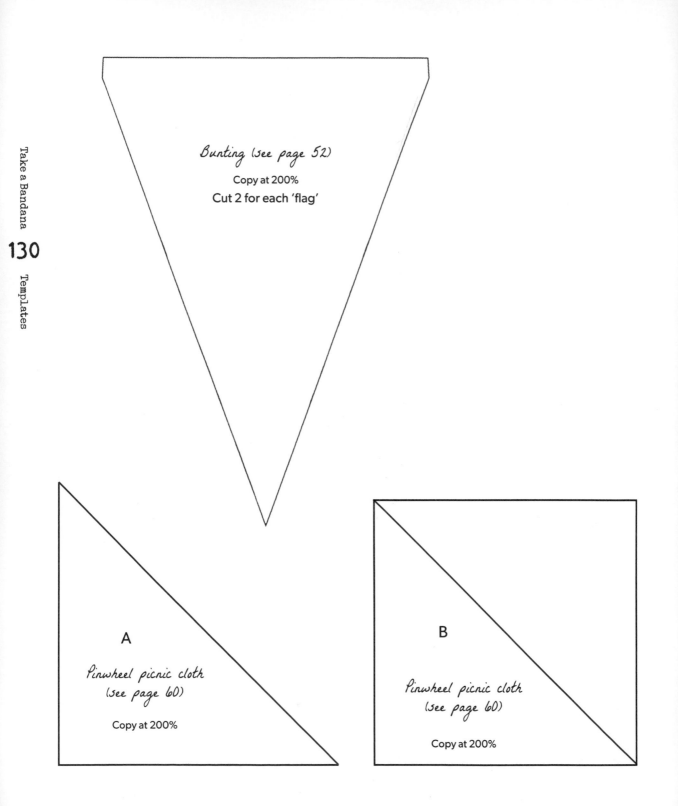

Bunting (see page 52)

Copy at 200%

Cut 2 for each 'flag'

A

Pinwheel picnic cloth
(see page 60)

Copy at 200%

B

Pinwheel picnic cloth
(see page 60)

Copy at 200%

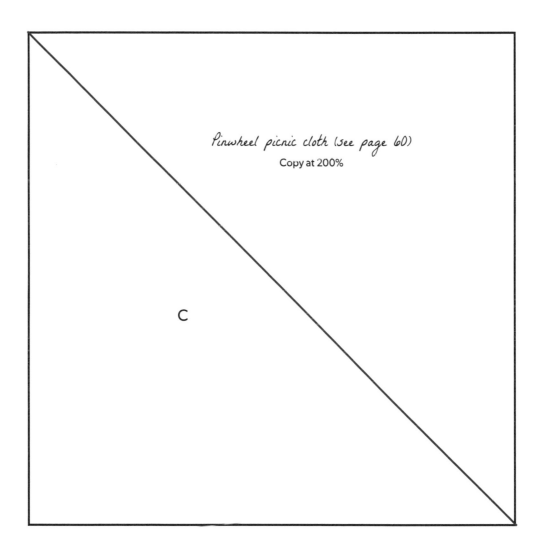

Pinwheel picnic cloth (see page 60)
Copy at 200%

C

Suppliers

ART SUPPLIES
Clarkes Office Supplies
www.clarkesofficesupplies.co.uk

BANDANAS
Bandana Shop
www.bandanashop.com

Dirty Harry
www.dirtyharryltd.com

To Be Worn Again
www.tobewornagain.co.uk

Hobby Lobby (US)
http://shop.hobbylobby.com

Only Bandanas (US)
www.onlybandanas.com

BAG HANDLES
Bag Clasps Ltd
www.bag-clasps.co.uk

CORD ELASTIC
Textile Garden
www.textilegarden.com

EMBROIDERY HOOPS
C & H Fabrics
www.candh.co.uk

THREADS, LINENS,
BUTTONS, FELT, TRIMS
AND TAPES
Brighton Sewing Centre
www.brightonsewingcentre.
co.uk

Coats Crafts
www.coatscrafts.com

John Lewis Partnership
www.johnlewis.com

Ditto Fabrics Ltd
www.dittofabrics.co.uk

NOTEBOOKS
Utility
www.utilitygreatbritain.co.uk

Acknowledgements

AUTHOR'S ACKNOWLEDGEMENTS Thanks to
Jonathan, Gilda, Virginia and Rebecca at GMC
and Andrew Perris for the beautiful photographs.
To Carolyn Clark for her quilting and to Val for
letting us shoot in her very special house. The most
thanks, of course, to my lovely family and friends.
Thank you. And finally, with happy memories of
stitching with Nathalie.

GMC PUBLICATIONS would like to thank:
Nicole for the loan of the vintage sewing machine,
Utility (www.utilitygreatbritain.co.uk) and The
White Company (www.thewhitecompany.com) for
the loan of other props.

Index

Page numbers in bold contain photographs of the completed projects.

To place an order, or to request a catalogue, contact:

GMC Publications Ltd, Castle Place, 166 High Street, Lewes, East Sussex, BN7 1XU, United Kingdom

Tel: +44 (0)1273 488005
www.gmcbooks.com